Do we still need the Ten Commandments?

Do we still need the Ten Commandments?

A Fresh Look at God's Laws of Love

JOHN H. TIMMERMAN

Augsburg
MINNEAPOLIS

For Patricia—who taught me the meaning

of these laws by living them daily

DO WE STILL NEED THE TEN COMMANDMENTS
A Fresh Look at God's Laws of Love

Acknowledgments: Brief portions of this book first appeared in different form in *Moody Monthly, The Banner, Christian Home 2 School,* and *The Reformed Journal.*

Cover Design by Ellen Maly
Text Design by Lois Stanfield, LightSource Images

ISBN 0-8066-2349-7

01   00   99   98   97   1   2   3   4   5   6   7   8   9   10

CONTENTS

Preface The Crossover   9

1 The True God   19

2 The False Gods   35

3 Loyalty to the One Who Loves You   51

4 Finding Rest in God   67

5 Putting Relationships in Order   81

6 Bearing the Image of God   101

7 Keeping Promises   111

8 Taking and Withholding   131

9 Telling the Truth   145

10 Learning to Be Satisfied   157

11 In the Potter's House   169

The Crossover

The Pilgrimage

The man and woman were dressed alike in hooded cloaks that were worn thin and bleached by sun and wind to a dull gray color. They stood uncertainly before the Sinai plain. The wind sawed over the grainy sand, flinging particles as fine as dust but as sharp as razors against their sandaled ankles. They squinted against the fiery eye of the rising sun.

The man leaned upon a shepherd's staff and watched the bowl of the plain fill with the wash of light. They stood on a slight rise, looking down upon the darker plain, and had to focus hard to make out the tents that seemed to ripple endlessly into the distance. Morning shadows clung to the edges of tents. In the still air, he heard an old man cough as he awakened. Somewhere two dogs quarreled over a scrap of food. The woman leaned against him and lifted one hand nervously to his arm.

He touched her fingers reassuringly, but his own hand, thick and rough from a life in the hills with the sheep, trembled involuntarily.

"So many people," he murmured.

She nodded. As far as she could see over the vast plain, tents sprawled in long spiraling circles. She felt it, too. They lived at the far fringes of this society, herding their sheep through the hills, always hunting for water or a bit of desert grass for the sheep to graze upon. They were unaccustomed to the press of people. They lived with spaces and silences. But it was not the people alone who made them afraid. They were going to meet the Lord.

Their eyes flickered again over the sea of tents, now washed white under the risen sun. Little puffs of smoke rose from cooking fires. Their eyes settled, finally, upon the large tent at the center of the twisting spiral.

The tent was huge, dwarfing all the others. Linen curtains hung from poles that fenced off the courtyard protectively. Sunlight leaked into the courtyard, and now, from their place on the rise, the man and woman could see thin smoke spiraling upward from the bronze altar in the courtyard. The wind seemed to lift the smoke toward them.

Drawing them or repelling them?

The man's hand trembled, and he felt the weight of the leash tethered to his wrist. The small lamb at his feet bleated uncertainly.

The man let his eyes rove past the altar. Behind it stood the tent of the tabernacle. Its goat-hide covering looked dull in the morning light. But inside, he had heard, under the goat hide, lay a linen covering, embroidered in scarlet and purple. That inner room, he had heard, dazzled with gold. It was a fearful place, a transportable palace for a king. Here the Lord himself dwelt. But they would not have to enter, he told himself. It was enough to approach the altar, to hand the lamb to the priest for a guilt offering, and then they—this shepherd Joel and his bride, Rachel—could be purified to begin their marriage in a holy way.

He sighed deeply, gathering his courage to move on. He had heard fearful tales of what lay within.

Bit by bit the stories had filtered out even to the wilderness hills where Joel and Rachel kept their sheep. They had never seen Moses, this man who talked with God. It was not their business to see such a man. But they had heard the stories . . . How Moses walked up the sacred mountain while its rocks were falling, the whole land trembling as some awful power shook it. Then the cloud, dense and thick as smoke, surrounded the mountain, and thunder and lightning shot from its flanks. And Moses walked right into it—none too eager, from what Rachel and Joel heard. But Moses did go up, and in the midst of the smoke and the blasting of thunder and crack of lightning, he talked with God.

And God told him to build . . . this. This tabernacle.

I wonder, Joel thought, *if Moses was as terrified to climb the mountain as I am to go to the tabernacle.*

Joel had heard other stories, too, about the Holy Place itself from other shepherds who had gone seeking a blessing.

In the forepart of the tent stood a golden table, upon which stood a golden lamp stand. Nearby, a small altar ceaselessly lifted sweet incense to the winds. The priests, robed in delicately colored linens inset with jewels, attended the Holy Place. What a thing it must be to walk in the place of the Lord.

Beyond the table—and here the stories had unnerved Joel completely—stood another, smaller tent—the Holy of Holies. The very place of the Lord! Here was kept the Ark of the Covenant containing the stone tablets on which God himself had carved his *word*.

A chest of rarest wood, overlaid with gold. As befits a king. And guardian figures, hammered out of pure gold. And in the ark—the *law* of the Lord.

Joel flicked a glance at Rachel. He gladly would have turned and left—right here, right now. Even after traveling all this way. But she smiled encouragement at him, her eyes dancing in the rising light. She tugged at his hand and pulled him forward. He wondered at the bravery of this woman he loved.

Then they were walking down the rise, toward the plain. The small lamb tugged against the leash. He bent, picked it up, and cradled it in his arms as they walked.

At least, he thought, *I don't have to go in there. The priests will do it—all of it—for me.*

The tent of the tabernacle seemed even larger as Joel and Rachel threaded their way through aisles of smaller tents, past cooking fires that filled the morning air with smoke, through people jostling for space on the crowded plain. So many people!

They had always known, of course, about this central grouping of their people, but their lives had been lived on the fringes, among the shepherds and cattlemen, far from this throng.

At last Joel and Rachel stood before the gates of the tabernacle, joining a small line of others bringing sacrifices. They found themselves trembling with excitement. And fear.

Someone else, Joel thought again, *will go into that place for me. I am not worthy to enter.*

Centuries have turned since that day when the young Israelite couple made their way, nervously yet expectantly, toward the tabernacle. They went expecting—wholly expecting—God to accept their sacrifice. They expected to meet God, however shrouded his glory might have been in the Holy of Holies and however far removed from their immediate contact.

In all of time's turning, pilgrims still come seeking God, desiring to find restoration into communion with him, wanting to find a revelation of order and peace for their lives in his holy will. Like the Israelite couple, Joel and Rachel, we are filled with the same conflicting emotions of fear and longing as we look for a way to approach God. But the truly amazing thing is that God longs for our approach. We draw near in fear; we are met with love.

In a sense, all has changed since that time when Joel and Rachel brought their guilt offering. The tabernacle was displaced by the temple and by synagogues; and, for Christians, the temple was displaced by the church. The Ark of the Covenant, its rich acacia wood overlaid with gold, is lost to all history. And despite the myths created by Hollywood, no one knows where God disposed of it. Or how.

All has changed.

And yet nothing has.

For modern pilgrims still come seeking that Holy of Holies, the place of God's presence, offering nothing less than their lives. The way into God's presence has changed, but the *experience* of God's presence remains the same—it still offers the revelation of his will for our lives.

The dramatic change lies in the way by which we come before God. None of us can keep his law perfectly. We all have turned from his will. None is worthy of entering God's presence. But we no longer need priests to prepare the way by offering the sacrifices we bring. From our side of history, we look at another man who stands on another hill. From the rise of that hill, he contemplated an awful sacrifice of restoration—nothing less than himself. More than the offering alone, Jesus is also the High Priest who mediates the offering that allows us to enter God's presence. The author of the New Testament book of Hebrews writes:

> *The point of what we are saying is this: We do have such a high priest, who sat down at the right hand of the throne of the Majesty in heaven, and who serves in the sanctuary, the true tabernacle set up by the Lord, not by man (Hebrews 8:1-2).*

The tabernacle, continues the writer, was merely "a copy and shadow of what is in heaven" (8:5). Jesus enacted the perfect sacrifice which was once and for all—and by means of which we are brought into the Holy of Holies—the presence of the living God. Because of this relationship, established by the perfect sacrifice of Jesus, the perfect High Priest, Saint Paul writes in his letter to the Christians in Rome that "I am convinced that neither death nor life, neither angels nor demons, neither the present nor the future, nor any powers, neither height nor depth, nor anything else in all creation, will be able to separate us from the love of God that is in Christ Jesus our Lord" (Romans 8:38-39).

Far from a fearful confrontation, we are brought into a loving relationship with the living God. And at the heart of this living relationship, no longer inscribed on tablets of stone but on the hearts of believers, lie the tenets of God's holy law *and* the power and grace of Jesus to live according to that law.

Modern Pilgrims

As we too seek this living and loving relationship with God, it is time to revitalize our theology and our Christian walk with God by a fresh examination and a reclaiming of the Ten Commandments. It is time to recover our relationship with God and to see in it God's amazing love for us.

To do this we must recognize, first of all, that the grace Jesus extends to us as the Son of God does not—mysteriously and suddenly—render God's commandments null and void. Jesus said that he came not to abolish the law and the prophets but to fulfill them (Matthew 5:17). The commandments cross over into modern history, interpreted and fulfilled by Jesus, and they are as pertinent to our spiritual lives today as they were the moment God spoke them amid thunder and smoke upon Mount Sinai.

Still, many people question why we would pay much attention to the Ten Commandments today. Oh, yes, they are all good in theory, some might say, but are they really necessary for Christians? After all, I'm not about to murder someone, and I haven't committed adultery. And I don't worship idols. And doesn't our salvation through Jesus, God's ultimate grace to us, surpass any set of laws? Am I not free, as a believer, to stop worrying about rules? Do we really need the Ten Commandments today?

These are not trivial questions. In fact, they elicit some profound answers that we will explore in the pages ahead. But it should be clear at the outset that there is a "specialness" about these commandments that has not diminished with time. One might call this specialness the unique blessings bestowed by obedience to God's laws. Each one outlines certain negative behaviors to avoid and implies their converse, *positive* behaviors to practice in order that we might have the benefit of a closer walk with God. Consider just a few of these benefits that will guide our study.

First, the Ten Commandments form a *practical* plan for Christian living. They are neither theoretical statements nor "good advice." They are specific, concrete guides that touch every area of our lives in direct and practical ways.

Second, the Ten Commandments are *authoritative*. In a world of confused and conflicting ideas, we can cling to these and say, "This is right." Why? Because their source is God. And now, in the present moment, God is speaking to us through them. In an age in which the term *values* has been so overused as to become nearly meaningless, we rightly yearn to anchor our values in God's unchanging rock of authority.

Third, the commandments are *relational*. Each commandment, as we shall see, positions us in a loving relationship with God who loves us. On the strength of the relationship with God, the commandments also guide us in all our earthly relationships. They fill the hole in our hearts that cries out for true and lasting love. They meet our need for tenderness, guide our friendships, give meaning to our interactions with family and neighbors. They offer healthy, fulfilling relationships because they establish, at the outset, a solid, loving relationship with God.

Fourth, the commandments are *eternal*, not historically bound by one period in time. They are gifts of God given to every age, given to *us*. Their source is the eternal God whose word is unchanging. We do not follow them because they are a kind of theological inheritance that the church passes along to believers. While the church ought to do this, clearly upholding and explaining the Ten Commandments to each new generation, they are appropriated individually into personal Christian living. The Ten Commandments form a deeply intimate expression of God's love for a redeemed people, but each person enters into his or her own personal love relationship with this God.

This book deals with the nuts and bolts of practical Christianity: the loving will of God. Such things are not erased by the cross of Christ. The crucifixion, rather, may be seen as a testimony of God's divine will and plan rather than as God changing his mind at some juncture in human history. Indeed, the crucifixion may be seen as a renewed emphasis, a crossover between two watersheds in human history—God's revelation of himself on Mount Sinai and God's revelation of himself on the hill of Golgotha. The essential nature of God does not change in the revelations. Both manifestations testify to the fact that he loves us dearly and has a design for our lives.

Although the intention of this study is to apply God's commandments to our daily living, an important historical matter warrants attention. In the history of the Christian church, different traditions of our common faith have arranged the commandments differently. For example, Lutheran, Catholic, and Episcopalian traditions list Deuteronomy 5:7 as the first commandment, and verses 8 through 10 as an appendix to it. Some later Protestant traditions divide these verses into two separate commandments. Another deviation in traditions occurs in Deuteronomy 5:21, where the ninth commandment appears as "You shall not covet your neighbor's house," and the tenth as "You shall not covet your neighbor's wife, or his manservant or maidservant, his ox or donkey, or anything that belongs to your neighbor." It is interesting from a historical perspective that while Martin Luther observes this division of the ninth and tenth commandments in his Large Catechism, he discusses them jointly, as do those traditions that treat the section on coveting as one commandment.

Regardless of how our traditions have numbered them, and for whatever reasons they have different numberings, the Ten Commandments are an essential unity that reveals God's will for Christian living. More, they reveal God's enduring, powerful love for his children and show us how we may, in turn, live in a loving relationship with him. This book is as much a study of God's *love* as it is of God's *law*.

The central message of this study of God's commandments—in their Old Testament revelation, their fulfillment in the New Testament revelation in Christ, and their significance to contemporary living—is simple: God still loves us dearly. His love is revealed by his will for our lives, a will for our protection and well-being revealed as much in his law given on Sinai as in his grace given on Golgotha. This is a study in first things: God's love for his people.

A word of caution must be added: love can be dangerous. A change of heart changes a way of living. In this regard, a biblically grounded Christian faith may be the most dangerous power in the world in its capacity to stop a life dead in its tracks, turn it around, and set it on a new course. God's love may set us free, but it is to a freedom controlled and guided by God. The claims of God that direct our freedom and offer us new life are remarkably few. Only ten.

1

The True God

I am the Lord your God,

who brought you out of Egypt,

out of the land of slavery.

You shall have no other gods before me.

EXODUS 20:2-3

It is essential at the outset of our study that we understand something about the God who has given us these laws and the love that lies behind his laws. In the opening words of the Ten Commandments, God speaks of his love before laying out his expectations. We will explore those words shortly. But God speaks of his love to us today as well. And he speaks in ways that are unique to our experiences—ways that are often unexpected, and ways that we may overlook at times. Perhaps a simple illustration from my own family's past will demonstrate how God's love can make itself felt in small and unexpected ways.

My wife and I hadn't known this particular store was sponsoring a "free, promotional giveaway," nor that what was being given away was goldfish. We were innocent shoppers until hooked by our two-year-old Joel's insistence upon having a goldfish. While Joel was wide-eyed with wonder at the little plastic bag with the dart of gold stabbing the water, we wondered on the way home whether we had any bowls left to house this fish. Or had the three older children, in their own series of turtles and fish, broken them all? Too many bowls had been knocked off a shelf by groping little fingers, winding up in a litter of broken glass, a spray of mossy marbles, and a sizable puddle of water.

What made Joel's goldfish different, perhaps, was the time at which we received it.

This was in June of 1987, when the airwaves sizzled with revelations of the Iran arms scandal, and the name of Lieutenant Colonel Oliver North was on the lips of practically everyone. We asked Joel what he wanted to name his goldfish. Following his older brother's prompting, he settled on "Colonel Ollie." Colonel Ollie it was.

The goldfish had at least one beneficial quality. Joel was an early riser and, whereas in former days he would shake his crib mercilessly while he called Mom or Dad from bed, we now found it strangely quiet in the morning. Joel stood, leaning on the rail of his crib, watching Colonel Ollie circle among the three colored stones that demarcated his underwater kingdom. Insofar as I know, no words passed between them; there was simply a fascination with this bright flash, this ounce of golden fish, scattering the morning sunshine in slightly murky water.

Colonel Ollie, like the popularity of his human namesake on the airwaves, thrived for his allotted span. Then one morning, the fish appeared more lethargic than usual, his tiny gills flapping, his circles more of a ragged stumble.

"Colonel Ollie's sick," my wife, Pat, said to Joel.

"Will he get better?"

"No, I don't think so."

By day's end, whatever spark had flickered in Colonel Ollie in the morning had disappeared. The goldfish was now destined for a ritual flush down the toilet. Despite its indelicacy, we have learned that this ceremony can nonetheless be significant. Pat walked with Joel and the goldfish bowl to the bathroom.

"Colonel Ollie is dead," she explained.

"Will he get better?"

"No. When someone dies, he doesn't get better."

"May I hold Colonel Ollie?" Joel asked.

"That wouldn't be a good idea," Pat said. "But you may touch him and then wave bye-bye when I flush him down the toilet."

Now, this was not a moment of solemn gravity, nor was it a moment of light-hearted jocularity. It was simply one of those moments that pass in a family. Joel waved, calling, "Bye-bye, Colonel Ollie," when Pat flushed the goldfish down the toilet. Joel watched the swirl, looked long and hard, and then said, "Colonel Ollie's gone now." And that was it. It was a simple act, one that we adults go through and forget and expect our children will forget also. One doesn't go in for heavy theology with a two-year-old at such a moment, explaining the difference between not seeing a goldfish again and the human death and resurrection. We thought it was the end of the matter.

But we had not reckoned on Roger.

Roger had become a dear friend of our family. In his mid-sixties, Roger had for years been unable to hold a steady job because of severe manic-depression. He was a kindly man, much appreciated by neighbors because in this busy world Roger always had time to stop and chat.

Twice a day, for years, Roger had walked around our block, a distance of nearly a mile. Our house being at the half-way point, it was not unusual for him to rap loudly at the door to ask if he could have a drink of water or use our bathroom. I think he really wanted to see Joel. They were madcap friends.

When two weeks passed late that summer without a visit from Roger, I stopped by the home of a widow at the corner to ask where he had been. Roger's mother, who lived in Kentucky, had died suddenly, and he had flown there for the funeral and to settle the estate. He was going to move to Kentucky. I asked the widow that, if she saw Roger again, would she please ask him to stop and say good-bye to us.

Two days later, in the evening, we heard his loud rap at the screen door and his voice calling. "Oh, Joel! Where's my buddy?" Roger came in and sat in the rocking chair. Pat sat on the sofa, and Joel played quietly on the floor with some of his cars.

When Pat asked Roger about his mother, he suddenly erupted into tears. Roger seldom does things quietly. This was a storm of tears, a cyclone.

Joel looked up from his cars and asked, "What's the matter with Roger?"

"Roger's very sad," Pat said. "His mother died."

"Oh," said Joel. He reflected a moment and asked, "Did he flush her down the toilet?"

"No," replied Pat. "Roger buried his mother in the ground."

"Never see her again?"

"Oh, yes. He'll see her again. Because his mother loved Jesus. She went to live with Jesus, and Roger will see her again."

Through Roger's sobs, Joel simply said, "Oh."

That was enough. Never mind that our oldest son was gasping with laughter in the other room. The connection had been made.

A moment of truth and a moment of faith. God's love penetrates our lives in the most commonplace and unexpected ways, from the coincidence of a "giveaway promotion," to an understanding of grace in which God gives us eternal life without our merit. So, too, God's love infiltrates our lives in the unexpected freedom that comes through his law.

Strange as it sounds, the Ten Commandments are all about freedom. As we approach the very first of God's laws, it is important to distinguish between two kinds of freedom. There is a freedom that ultimately confines us to the world of our own choices, and there is one that liberates us by the commandments of the God who has made this world. The distinction between the two is complex. Often we wish to barter, keeping certain areas of our life protected and subject to our own choices. The tricky part is that God's commandments break into and expose those areas, and, in doing so, give us true freedom. To understand God's law is also to understand his love and his grace. To understand God's love and grace is to understand our ultimate freedom.

This seems, at first glance, a contradiction. To the modern mind, any law appears to limit personal freedom. Since the law is imposed by an authority, whether it be an individual, a corporation, or a civil body, it suggests that our relationship to that authority consists of simple obedience. Certain rewards often accrue to the obedient one—security, peace, or harmony—but these are the result of our obedience to some higher master. The relationship seems a bit cold and mechanical. In contrast, grace suggests a relationship founded upon love and deep intimacy. It suggests two parties meeting together in mutual love and concern. How, then, can we speak of the law as a way in which God offers his love and blessings?

Before a loving relationship can exist, both parties must know each other well. There can be no surprises or reservations in that relationship. To understand how God's law is also a revelation of his love and grace, it is important to explore the first commandment, which reveals the nature of the two parties involved: God and humanity.

The introduction to the commandments in Exodus 20:2 opens with a grand and sweeping announcement of who God is. It's as if God shouts, "Here I am! I love you!" Here God takes the first step in the action of love: he reveals himself in a name: "I am the Lord—*Jehovah.*" And, more than this, "I am *your God.*" Then God reminds his people of his love with a further description: "who brought you out of Egypt, out of the land of slavery." These are descriptions, statements of identity. The commandment "You shall have no other gods before me" follows.

The Israelites lived as God's chosen people in a culture marked by polytheism and idolatry. The people all around them served many gods: they had a god for crops, a god for household affairs, for good weather, for curses or blessings, for war, for peace. They were a busy people, keeping all those gods satisfied. And it was also very confusing. Who finally rules? Who has final say? Who bears authority? The people must have gone wild worshiping all their gods.

Because there was never a sense of final, absolute authority, there was also never a sense of final, absolute satisfaction. How much do I give to one god? How much to another? And so the people, trying nervously to satisfy all the powers, never really knew peace.

In fact, they often perverted and corrupted peace. One group of people had made a metal representation of a god called Molech. The statue was hollow on the inside.

The people would kindle a hot fire inside the statue so that the metal glowed. Then, to appease Molech, they laid their children on the outstretched arms of the statue, and the children were seared to death by the intense heat. The polytheistic people could never give enough because they never knew who the true god was at any given time.

The True God

That context is important because the commandment has to do with worship. In the ancient Greek and Hebrew the word *worship* meant literally "to fall down before," or "to revere." Much of that meaning remains in modern use of the word. The problem in ancient times, with all the gods being heralded for prominence, was the question of which god— if any—was worthy of true and solitary worship.

These gods were invented by humans to meet human needs, in humanity's image. Certain sacrifices, these people believed, would persuade the gods to respond to those human needs. Humans tried to manipulate the divine powers for their own advantage. Never was there a personal relationship between god and humans; always it was an issue of power.

It would also be accurate to describe these religions as a kind of devil worship. Satan's oldest and cleverest lie is the promise of satisfaction for human desires: *You can get what you want if only you . . .* Therefore, one of the strongest cautions threading throughout the Old Testament is against consulting mediums, or wizards, or any human intermediaries claiming to have divine powers. All these were attempts to manipulate divine powers to serve human desires. Satan tempts us to immediate answers rather than to faithful obedience.

It is a common temptation to seek other gods, and one not limited to Old Testament people. It roots in the very nature of a fallen humanity. In this commandment God directly calls our attention to this temptation. He knows us. He names our need here: the need for an authoritative, living Lord.

Repeatedly one finds in Scripture this emphasis upon serving the one living God and proscriptions against serving supernatural powers other than God. Over and over, God reminds the people, as he does here, "*I am the Lord your God.*"

This point is foundational to our understanding of all of the commandments. In a polytheistic culture, God announces to his people: "I am the Lord your God." We understand several things by this. First, instead of many gods, there is one God. Second, this one God bears a name. He is the Lord—Jehovah, the Creator God, the God omnipotent, above and before all the gods of Satan's cunning design. Third, this God is *your* God.

There is remarkable comfort in that last phrase: *your God.* It is as if God is saying, "I have chosen to reveal myself, and my will, to you. I love you so much that I have called you to be *my* people and I am your God." We have here a deeply personal, loving relationship in which humans don't have to cry out to some remote deity, but instead find *themselves* called by an all-powerful God who reveals himself in love. That's the wonderful invitation that heads all the commandments: "I am God Almighty. I love you. You are my people. Therefore I reveal my will for you in these commandments to keep our relationship loving and undefiled."

As evidence of that love, God reminds the Israelites what he did for them in the past: "I brought you out of slavery." The people have been set free, not to be slaves to one more tyrant, but to love and worship a God who loves them. "How do we do this?" the people might wonder. God tells them in the commandments—beginning with the first one: "You shall have no other gods before me."

Witchcraft and the Living God

In the light of that dramatic revelation and commandment, it is stunning that the Israelites so frequently turned to their dark obsession with witchcraft. Scripture ripples with warnings to them and to us. Leviticus 19:26, for example, places a clear injunction against witchcraft: "Do not practice divination or sorcery." The same caution is made in Leviticus 19:31, "Do not turn to mediums or seek out spiritists, for you will be defiled by them: I am the Lord your God." The next chapter starts with a warning about the false god Molech; then in verse 6, God says, "I will set my face against the person who turns to mediums and spiritists to prostitute himself by following them, and I will cut him off from his people." And the chapter concludes in verse 27, "A man or woman who is a medium or spiritist among you must be put to death." Each time the Lord mentions this, he also points out something like "I the Lord am holy" or "I am the Lord your God." In all such pronouncements God asks his people to trust in his power and sovereignty rather than to seek immediate satisfaction from worldly sources.

The Israelites turned from the eternal commandments in their search for immediate answers. Instead of a simple obedience, they wanted to work out their own solutions, to "make deals" with the Devil. But while we stand stunned at the Israelites' folly, we also have to confess that the supernatural power of the occult is very much alive today. We are still engaged in a struggle to work out our own deals, find our own answers. Certainly these struggles may take a different shape from consulting occultic wizards and mediums. They are just as likely to involve the more subtle gods of wealth, power, and empty "spirituality," for example. That charges the commandment "You shall have no other gods before me" with powerful emphasis. An example from the modern church may demonstrate the point.

Defeating Dragons

The popular Christian apologist C. S. Lewis wrote that those who want to embrace a life-changing Christian faith must somehow make their way past "watchful dragons." These wrathful creatures are the guardians of propriety in the church, the bastions of church order. They insist that things belong in their place. They treasure tradition at all costs. Their rules slam cell-doors upon individual expression, upon meaningful personal worship. Above all, they loathe change.

Under the reign of the watchful dragons, our spiritual lives are reduced to fearful whispers and empty rituals. We mouth our liturgies and stifle our spirits. Church, and even faith, become hollow shells devoid of life. This is religion without effort—a follow-the-leader experience in mindlessness. In this, we are not unlike the ancient Israelites. We—church organizations, too—want a god that requires no commitment of us, one we can quickly understand and manipulate. We will go through the Sunday rituals because we hope thereby to appease God, to keep on his good side, just in case we ever should need his help. But please don't ask us to break out of those rituals in order to struggle into a serious personal relationship of love and obedience.

This is idolatry. We have made God into a god.

As someone who has had a lifelong love for exercise and athletics, I have observed a curious parallel between physical and spiritual fitness. Becoming fit takes time and effort, pure and simple. There are so many times when I just plain have to talk myself into that run, or the weight room, or the racquetball game. And I begin to wonder about all the shortcuts touted in advertising. Maybe there is a simpler way . . .

Holistic health offers techniques ranging from iridology to yoga to Rolfing. Health food stores, while predicated upon the worthy principle that our diets need reshaping, often fill their counters with dubious products ranging from processed seaweed to "amino assets" that claim "miracle health cures"— and in the process, the stores also fill their cash registers. All of us are eager to find shortcuts to good health, ways that don't require much effort.

Leaving church one Sunday morning, I saw yellow flyers tucked under the windshield wiper of every car on our parking lot. Since I don't drive to church, I had to liberate one from someone else's car. The flyer was an ad for healing by a spiritualist. The irony of finding these ads on the church parking lot is enough to make one weep. "GOD SENT— GOD'S MESSENGER" announced the brochure. Among its promises to rid one's home of "Hoo Doo," cure alcoholism, and restore "Lost Nature," the brochure for Sister Mary's healing service proclaimed:

> *The Religious Holy Woman healer, God's messenger, guarantees to heal the sick and the ailing, to remove all suffering and bad luck from your body. She is a religious and holy woman who will show you with your own eyes how she will remove sorrow, sickness and pain, and all bad luck. What your eyes see, your heart must believe. The Power to Heal by Prayer. Are you suffering? Are you sick? Do you need help?*

Best of all, Sister Mary's services, the brochure promised, are guaranteed. You just have to pay her a visit and (strongly suggested) cross her palm with silver. The example of Sister Mary and her "guaranteed healing" demonstrates how human need can give rise to a search for quick answers. And the quickest answers are usually supplied by Satan in his efforts to turn us from God's will to our own devices. Anything that transfers our trust in God to some other power is idolatry and a violation of the first commandment.

We are to repudiate anything that leads us from God. That's the heart of the first commandment. All other sins follow from that first turning from God. The commandment tells us to keep our eyes on God, to make him the focus of our life. That puts God before our own desires, before temptations, before anything else. In the same way that all sins follow from turning our backs on God, all blessings and all freedom follow from focusing upon God.

In 2 Chronicles 7:14, the Old Testament says, "If my people, who are called by my name, will humble themselves and pray and seek my face and turn from their wicked ways, then I will hear from heaven and will forgive their sin and will heal their land." This wonderful message of hope was repeated over and over by the ancient prophets, as they called God's people back to righteousness.

The same call to righteousness appears in the New Testament as well. Jesus repeatedly urges his listeners to worship the true God. In the Gospel of John, Jesus announces: "Now is the time for judgment on this world, now the prince of this world"—by which he means Satan—"will be driven out. . . . For I did not speak of my own accord, but the Father who sent me commanded me what to say and how to say it. I know that his command leads to eternal life" (from John 12:31-50).

God calls us to worship no one but him in this commandment, and he compels us to confront the hard question of where we place our trust—in ourselves or in God. It may seem an easy question to respond to, yet we are not so easily off the hook. Basically, we *can choose* what or who we will worship. God has given us that choice, else our worship is not worthy. If we choose to worship money or sex or power or anything other than the true God, what we really choose are our own desires and ambitions—ourselves, in other words.

The basic choice in our lives, then, is this: the worship of God or the idolatry of self. There is no greater divide in all of religion, and that's why this commandment *has* to come first. "Choose you this day whom you will serve," Moses said to the Hebrews of old. The decision is ours, as well.

The greatest threat to true religion today may be the cult of the individual. More than ever, we are led to believe that if it feels good or right, we should do it. The religion of Dr. Feelgood, or Do-Your-Own-Thing, is the modern form of idolatry. The terrible reality of Christianity is that we are free to choose. Free from bondage; free to worship God. But also free to choose the designs of our own minds over obedience to the living God. The instruction of this commandment is that there is only one genuine freedom, and that comes from choosing God.

Worshiping the true God involves total faith and trust in a being far beyond our comprehension. This is not a God who can be formed in our image, bounded by the strictures of our traditions, liturgies, or personal desires. We come to know God better, to grow in our relationship with him, only as we put him first in our lives and follow him.

REFLECTIONS

1. Take a minute to consider your thoughts about God's law. What feelings come to mind when you think of the Ten Commandments? Are they negative or positive? What, if any, role do the commandments play in your life? How do you think most people view the Ten Commandments today?

   Strange as it may seem, studies indicate that most people *like* rules. Most people are looking for authority or guidance in their lives. Is this true for you? What lies behind this attitude?

2. The emphasis throughout this study of the Ten Commandments is God's overwhelming love for us. Stop for a moment to consider the word "love." Love always occurs within *relationships*: we love others, others love us. What do we mean when we say we love others? List qualities that define our love for others.

   Even more mysterious, perhaps, is why others love us. This is a mystery often touched by grace, rather than one that can be explained clearly or rationally. Instead of asking what there is about us that draws someone's love, consider *what happens* when someone loves us. What are qualities of that love? What are its effects on us?

3. How does the story about the "free, promotional giveaway" typify the evangelism methods employed by some religious movements? Is this a good or bad approach?

   Is there such a thing as a "free giveaway" in any religion, or does religion always demand some kind of payment?

Do you think there is a cost to Christianity? What is it, and how has it been paid? What does it cost you?

4. The commandments open with a grand and sweeping announcement: "I am the Lord your God, who brought you out of Egypt, out of the land of slavery." This is a statement of identity, a description. Read the opening part of that announcement aloud to yourself. How does it feel to hear God say: "I am the Lord *your* God"?

   How would you change the second part of God's announcement—"who brought you out of Egypt, out of the land of slavery"—to describe God's past relationship with you? Would your description also include the phrase "who brought you . . . out of the land of slavery"?

5. Under the section **Defeating Dragons**, the author explains: "We will go through the Sunday rituals because we hope thereby to appease God, to keep on his good side, just in case we ever should need his help. . . . This is idolatry. We have made God into a god."

   In what sense is this attitude idolatry? What is the "idol" that we have created?

6. The concluding paragraph of this chapter offers two interesting insights: "Worshiping the true God involves total faith and trust in a being far beyond our comprehension. . . . We come to know God better . . . only as we put him first in our lives and follow him."

   How is "coming to know God better" different from "comprehending" God?

2

The False Gods

You shall not make for yourself an idol

in the form of anything in heaven above

or on the earth beneath or in the waters below.

You shall not bow down to them or worship them;

for I the Lord your God, am a jealous God,

punishing the children for the sin of the fathers

to the third and fourth generation

of those who hate me,

but showing love to thousands who love me

and keep my commandments.

EXODUS 20:4-6

The first chapter, focusing on the commandment to have no other gods before the one, true God, tells us to whom our worship is due. The three verses that follow that commandment—Exodus 20: 4-6— expand on and clarify our obligations to God and the response we can expect, in turn, from him.

In their consideration of these verses, however, two Christian traditions differ. Catholic, Lutheran, and Episcopal traditions, for example, treat them as an appendix to the first commandment. Martin Luther, in his Large Catechism, discusses them as such, within the context of the first commandment. Later Protestant traditions separate these verses into a separate commandment that stipulates some conditions of worship and bans others. An essential unity, however, is clear in both interpretations. Humanity has an instinct or need to worship; whom or what we choose to worship is the issue addressed by God.

The first commandment responds to that craving for worship that God gifted us with. It is a remarkable gift, a gateway that opens onto eternal life—or, if it is misdirected, onto eternal death. The commandment guides and directs our worship rightly, but it also anticipates the problem for humanity. Our natural—or fallen—desires lead us to worship things other than God. These verses specifically address this fact, and reveal practical implications that are as pertinent to us today as they were to the Israelites thousands of years ago.

Why Do People Worship Idols?

The Israelites, we remember, were a called people, a chosen nation. God announces that he is their God, and he claims them as his chosen people. He tells them that he alone is worthy of worship. He reminds them of his love and tells them how to worship him. And yet God's Old Testament people repeatedly turn away from God to worship idols.

Idolatry infiltrated Israelite worship like a virulent illness. Some people committed idolatry by worshiping the golden calf at the foot of the very mountain from which God's commandments were issued. Later, as they crossed into the promised land, God's people joined their new neighbors, the Canaanites, in the evil worship of Baal. And so it continued throughout Old Testament history. And so, too, it continues into the present. Many of us are dangerously close to those wayward Israelites, looking for our own golden calf or Canaanite deity.

What is there about human nature that turns us away from God to pursue the idols of our own making or those of our neighbors? Why would one want to worship idols? If we can identify that impulse, that reason, we may be able better to avoid it.

1. The Religious Instinct in Humanity

A young African-American student recently wrote an essay about black gospel music in one of my courses. It was an excellent essay, and I had the opportunity to talk with him about it. His remarks struck me so powerfully that afterward I jotted them down. They are enlightening of the issue here.

"In high school," he said, "I did a study of my roots, tracing the family history. It was a big thing then in schools. I started talking with my classmates about blacks as a people, a family in their own right. About our common ancestry. I wasn't a Christian at the time, but I saw how religion has been a tremendously important part of the black experience. Not always a positive one, though—at least not when it involved the white man's religion."

I asked him why that was so.

"The answer to that," he observed, "should be obvious. For many, Christianity was associated with slavery. You see, many of the slaves had to go to the white man's service on Sunday morning. And the white preacher would preach to them. The slaves always sat in the balcony. And the text was always the same."

"Let me guess," I said. "'Slaves obey your masters.'"

"Right. But in the evenings the slaves held their own services down by the woods. They had ring-shout, preaching, healing, and especially singing. The songs were the spirituals, the subject of my essay. They were highly symbolic. 'All God's Children Got Shoes.' Well, a slave might get a pair of shoes as a Christmas present from the plantation owner. But those wore out by March or April. So they did their plowing and field work barefoot. They longed for something as simple as shoes, which represented freedom for them. And 'Swing Low, Sweet Chariot' refers to Elijah's fiery chariot, but to the slaves it also stood for liberation from a life of oppression. This kind of religion, these spirituals, were an important part of my people, of what it means to be black. My people *had* to worship. It was *their spirit* reaching higher than slavery."

"I see what you mean. There is a longing for the divine in God's creation—for something better, something more than the troubles in this life."

"That, but more than that. You see, even on the streets there is a kind of law of retribution. Sometimes it's something like, 'You do me harm; I'll get my brothers and harm you back.' But there is a law that wrongs would be avenged. The slaves also believed that their oppressors would be punished, even if they couldn't do it themselves. Even if it happened after they were dead."

A general "religious" feeling dwells in people, by which they appeal to a divine source for help, for justice, for a better world. Maybe for some this is nothing more than a "Higher Power." Maybe for others it's a kind of grotesque power-broker, an avenger in a black leather jacket and brass knuckles. But humans have an instinct of morality and justice—a system of "oughtness"—and of some power beyond ourselves that will enforce that system.

The concept of the religious instinct suggests that part of being human is recognition of some divine authority. Some psychological approaches dismiss this instinct as a self-projection or wish-fulfillment syndrome, and some pop-theological approaches abuse this instinct as a recognition of the divine force within human personality. Christian theology recognizes it as the traces of God's image, or what is called the *Imago Dei,* within us. In its simplest terms, the image of God means that because humans were created in the image of God (Genesis 1:26), each of us possesses a fundamental awareness of God. We were created *like* God, and even though through sin we have fallen away from that likeness, we still have in us an awareness of divine power. And, no matter how obscured or distorted it may have become, this awareness creates in us a longing—a need—to worship.

2. The Desire to Manipulate God

This religious instinct in people also allies with the fact that idolatry satisfies a desire for psychological manipulation. Idolatry allows people a false sense that they can wield a degree of power over the divine, thereby providing some personal satisfaction or fueling a lust for power. This belief is based on the idea that God is really a projection of ourselves, or that we are ourselves all parts of some divine world-spirit we call God. The idea runs like a crooked river through much of nineteenth-century American literature. For example, Ralph Waldo Emerson, a leader in transcendentalism, said that we are all "sparks of a cosmic fire" called divine. But the concept neither began nor stopped with transcendentalism. It traces back to the works of Plato in ancient philosophy, and is still present today in many forms of New Age thought. In the twentieth century, Erich Fromm wrote a book called *Psychoanalysis and Religion,* in which he describes religion as a psychological projection. If we project, or envision, a god from our own psychological need, then we are ultimately in control of that God. Fromm maintains that we give too much psychological control over to the Christian God and that we should reclaim it for ourselves. In his book he writes, "Inasmuch as humanistic religions are theistic, God is a symbol of man's own powers which he tries to realize in his life, and is not a symbol of force and domination, having power over man."

It may well be that humanistic religions project a god who symbolizes human power. Humanism is in fact nothing less than the deification of human power. Dancing its celebration of human achievement, humanism inevitably trips over human failure; it stumbles upon discouragement; it clogs down in illness, pain, loneliness, and loss. For this, humanism has no means of accounting; powerless humans have no place in a theology of human power. Worship of one's own power is a risky enterprise. And whenever we seek to manipulate the divine—whether that means the gods we have created or God himself—we are projecting our own human understandings and desires onto God. We are playing at being God. And that indeed is risky.

3. A Need for a Visible God

Idolatry debases the divine by trying to capture God in a concrete, visible form. For example, God is revealed through nature and may be seen in and through his creation, but to worship that creation as the Creator is as foolish as playing the first three notes of Handel's *Messiah* and saying you have thereby captured either Handel or the *Messiah*. Idolatry sees God captured and confined in the thing. People want a god they can see, so they fashion an image—of wood, or metal, or stone—and call this thing "God." People today craft visible gods out of possessions or friends or pop stars—materials that may at first seem more sophisticated than ancient idols served by the Israelites, but materials that are equally base and fallible. In this misguided effort we are no different from the Israelites to whom God first spoke these words. Place yourself back in their time for a moment. God's Old Testament people lived in a land marked by ever-changing and fascinating landscapes. Even the desert of Sinai was far from a flat wasteland. The land ripples, collides against strange and majestic rocky buttes, holds surprises of greenery stitched through dry and wind-blasted valleys. The daytime sky is often of a clarity so intense and pure it hurts the eye; ruffled bands of cloud float overhead against the crystal blue sky. At night the stars dance just beyond reach.

Yet the biblical record of the Israelites' desert wandering seems almost to ignore the visual panorama. In all the scriptural passages of the Exodus, precious little visual imagery or description appear. Instead, the focus is on sound: the Israelites were a people attuned to hearing. Images of sound, passages of listening, everywhere mark their story.

The pattern is most pronounced in the extraordinary revelation of God at Mount Sinai. The description in Exodus 19 is of an almost exclusively auditory event. All the people could bear to see was a dense, veiling cloud crackling with bolts of lightning. What they heard, however, was a cataclysm of sound—thunder rocked the mountain ("the mountain trembled violently"), and blasts of a trumpet rose louder and louder. One way of interpreting the original Hebrew that describes the Sinai setting is that the people "saw the sound." The descriptive imagery of the Exodus passage relates directly to the nature of God's method of revealing himself.

The people of the plains—pagan nations surrounding the Israelites—worshiped gods they could see, idols shaped by their hands. But Israel worshiped the God of the mountain, whose living voice spoke to them through peals of thunder and blasts of the trumpet. No human eye could confine this God to a visual image.

God calls to his people, "Hear, O Israel," "Hearken, my people," "Listen to the words of the Lord your God." And so, too, the Ten Commandments were spoken by God as the authoritative will of the most High Lord, the God of the Mountain.

DO WE STILL NEED THE TEN COMMANDMENTS?

Search this further, for herein also lies the miracle of God's love. The God of the Mountain, veiled in dense cloud and peals of thunder that drove the Israelites to their knees, called out to his people to tell them how to live in love. What other god has ever done this? Other gods are remote, distant, silent. Here is a God who calls out to his people.

Now take it one step further: this same God also responded to the human longing to *see* God. He manifested himself in Jesus. In a mystery so profound that we can only attach those familiar theological terms—incarnation, virgin birth, Messiah—to it, the God of the Mountain willingly became human. God took on the very human flesh that could not see God, but in this mystery *became* God for all to see. El Elyon, *most High God*; but also Immanuel, *God with us*.

So we see that this human longing for a visible God was in fact fulfilled in Jesus. Even so, people still turn to the physical present, to a visible god of their own making, rather than to the eternal reality of Jesus. They want to worship the here and now—a third reason for idolatry. But there may be a fourth reason yet why people insist upon idolatry.

4. A Confused Sense of Freedom

Some people, following their own desires rather than God's will, believe they are choosing freedom. Idolatry represents freedom for them. "I won't be bound by the laws of someone else. I'll choose my own way," expresses a common attitude. The question is: Is this really freedom?

Perhaps one could respond with an old metaphor of a train journey. It goes like this. If a train wants to get to Chicago, it has the freedom to follow the tracks, thereby eventually arriving in Chicago. If it chooses to leave the tracks, seeing freedom as doing whatever it wants, it may well wind up in a cornfield, going precisely nowhere.

Every freedom is attended by responsibilities if its aim is to reach a goal. No responsibility at all is also no freedom at all, for then one simply wanders aimlessly. Essentially, idolatry purports to be a freedom by which one chooses one's own way through life. But this is a choice that leads nowhere and finds nothing at all. That's a false sense of freedom.

In William Golding's book *Lord of the Flies*, a plane filled with choir boys crash-lands on an island. The first thing the boys do is to celebrate an apparent absence of rules. They are freed from any adult governance or interference. So they make their own rules, enjoying, they believe, a completely existential freedom. The island seems a paradise of freedom to them at first—but with humans playing God, it becomes dangerously destructive. All order disappears as each boy wants to go his own way.

It also becomes increasingly demonic. The fly-infested head of a pig they have slaughtered becomes their totem, their idol. The book's very title, *Lord of the Flies*, is a translation of the Hebrew name for Satan, *Beelzebub*.

Existential freedom, or freedom of the self, always makes things relative to a time or place. It seems to be freedom because it speaks to the moment; it is governed by one's immediate desires and feelings. But it is actually enslavement to the present and to our fallen nature.

Conversely, true freedom flows from following some eternal, timeless law in which we find directions that apply to every age. It originates not in time-relative, self-made autonomy, but in an absolute authority.

We call such an authority *God*. And we find it through the Authority's revelation of himself, in the Bible. And that Authority's guidelines for right actions—actions which offer true freedom—lie in the Ten Commandments.

These four human characteristics that lead to idolatry are manifested in many different ways in our own lives. Idolatry is not simply an act that belongs to the "heathen others." It lurks in our own hearts. The words of Exodus 20:4-6 confront each believer, driving us to our knees before the question: Whom do you serve?

✓   Those four characteristics can help us examine our relationship with God and provide a clearer focus in our worship of him. If there lies in each of us a "religious instinct" to worship, what have we done with it? Have we located that "longing for God" in our lives? Have we dared to admit it? Have we nurtured and directed it? Or have we subverted it under layers of demands and the busyness of daily living?

Each of us is called by this commandment to carve out an essential portion of our daily living to wholeheartedly nurture this part of our human nature. Each of us has to find his or her individual rhythms for communion with God. But, if we are to take seriously this first and foremost commandment, each believer will adopt some pattern of daily worship. The alternative is clear: the instinct will not be denied, and if it is not directed to the true God, it will lead to idolatry and despair.

✓   The second reason can be equally instructive—the desire to manipulate God. Christianity is about authority—the basis for love-actions—it is never about power or manipulation. All too often, however, we let the noisy sounds of power-claims insinuate their clamor into our lives.

Consider how this may occur subtly. How much of our prayer life is directed toward our own ends rather than toward service for God? Too often we voice only a litany of personal wishes before the throne of God. Instead of adoration, we want things. Instead of direction for humble servant-hood, we desire comforts. In fact, God already has met our needs, is currently meeting our needs, and will meet all the needs that our future may unfold. His promises have not diminished one whit in all of time's turning. His promise, "Do not fear, for I am with you; do not be dismayed, for I am your God. I will strengthen you and help you; I will uphold you with my righteous right hand" (Isaiah 41:10), is ever with us, whatever our desires or needs.

Consider how the need to manipulate may occur overtly. Too often our modern congregations are locked in power struggles. Conflicts rage over preaching styles, traditional versus contemporary styles of worship and music; over outreach to our communities versus programs to meet the needs of the congregation. While each struggle is well worth consideration for any church's mission, too often these become simply power struggles in the church. Christianity is not, has never been, nor ever should be, about power. If anything, it is about powerlessness, our need and task before the authority of God.

In the second area we also do well to examine our own hearts. Search that territory for signs of personal manipulation of God, or a struggle for power at the cost of humble obedience. Each area broaches the terrain of idolatry.

✓ The third human trait that can lead to idolatry—a need for a visible God—may, perhaps, most easily be understood by us. How readily we worship the things we see, particularly when we declare them ours. It is not a huge step to place tangible possessions in the place of God. Nor is it unlikely to find ourselves in bondage to such possessions.

It is a condition of the heart endemic to the very blessings of this nation we enjoy. Having so much, being so richly blessed by God, we often begin to worship the gift rather than the giver.

If our lives are spent in the acquisition of things, we are emptying our days in an absurd bank account of idolatry. And this is a bank that can never be filled; with each deposit, we will be driven to acquire more.

There is an easy corrective if we think of the days of our lives as an investment account, rather than a vault to store possessions. Then we can concentrate on investments that will grow and offer dividends: worship of God, service to God and to others.

I knew one such investment broker. She labored tirelessly to enrich the lives of others. In a thousand quiet ways she invested her hours in service under God. Whether reading to her children and nurturing them in faith, or carrying home-baked goodies to those who had far too little, or teaching

Bible classes to those craving the truth, she worshiped God in daily living. When this woman, my mother, died recently, a poem by the Christian poet Christina Rossetti was read at her funeral. The concluding lines of "Weary in Well-Doing" are:

I go, Lord, where Thou sendest me;
Day after day I plod and moil:
But, Christ my Lord, when will it be
That I may let alone my toil
And rest in Thee?

When, one gray evening, I had to tell my parents that the terrible weeks of chemotherapy and radiation had had no effect on the cancer attacking her body, that in fact her cancer had only grown worse, Mom appeared strangely calm. She knew, you see. She turned to me and asked, "How much longer do I have to live?" I had asked the same question of her doctors, and I replied with the answer they gave me. "The doctors just don't know, Mom. Maybe several months." She died precisely three weeks later. I should have given a different answer. I should have said, "Forever, Mom. Forever." But *she* knew.

Finally, we also do well to measure our worship of God by examining our own concept of freedom. A good way to explore this issue is by answering these questions: What causes you the most stress? Your quiet moments in prayer? Or the demands of the world?

A close friend of mine, and a member of the Bible study group I have been in for years, has worked all his life as a counselor. He is a wonderful counselor, one who spends time in prayer before every session and one who seeks genuinely biblical solutions to the most terrible psychological traumas people bring into his office. And he is a thoroughly realistic counselor. In fact, we sometimes jokingly refer to his agency as "The Down-to-Earth Counseling Corporation." The heart of his realism, however, lies in his belief that people will not acquire holistic psychological health until they locate it in God.

In the course of his career, he has observed that nearly every problem he confronts, with the exception of biochemically induced mental illnesses, originates in a person's turning from God to choices contrary to God's will. Often the problems result from choices made from a misguided sense of personal freedom.

A virtual cult of "personal freedom" has captured the American mind. In it, the "I" is held up as deity, supreme arbiter of values. If it is right for me, the belief goes, it is just plain right. The problem is that the whole premise is wrong. It suborns the human religious instinct into worship of self; it makes of free choice an end in itself. Freedom without authoritative direction will always shipwreck into the counselor's office, where people like my friend try to glue the rubble back together. Such repair work is impossible without a miracle of God's grace—and that miracle begins in worshiping the Lord our God, finding again his "steadfast love to thousands of those who love me and keep my commandments."

REFLECTIONS

1. What are the most "popular" idols that people worship in today's world? What forms does this worship take?

Why do people set up these idols—what needs are being met by such false gods?

What sacrifices or "tribute" do the idols in our life demand?

2. Four reasons why people create idols, the author notes, are 1) the religious instinct in humanity, 2) the desire to manipulate God, 3) a need for a visible god, and 4) a confused sense of freedom.

Which, if any, of these characteristics do you recognize from your own experiences?

3. In the story of the African-American student's comments about slavery and religion is the observation that "even on the streets there is a kind of law of retribution . . . a law that wrongs would be avenged. The slaves also believed that their oppressors would be punished, even if they couldn't do it themselves. Even if it happened after they were dead."

How does such an attitude indicate a "religious instinct" or a belief in a god? What kind of "god" is reflected by this attitude? Is this attitude common even among Christians?

4. The section **A Need for a Visible God** begins with the words "Idolatry debases the divine by trying to capture

God in a concrete, visible form." Why do you think humans have wanted a God whom they could see?

How does this desire for a visible god relate to the desire to manipulate God?

5. According to the author, God has chosen to reveal himself to us through sounds and words—the thunderous sounds at Sinai, the words of the Ten Commandments, the messages of the prophets. What does this means of revelation say about our relationship with God? About our ways of worshiping?

6. One way of examining our own lives for signs of manipulating God is by assessing our prayers to God: "How much of our prayer life is directed toward our own ends rather than toward service to God?" How would you answer that question?

Is it wrong to pray for our own needs and desires? What makes the difference between selfish, self-centered prayers and prayers that acknowledge God's rule and direction?

3

Loyalty to the One Who Loves You

You shall not misuse the name

of the Lord your God,

for the Lord will not hold anyone guiltless

who misuses his name.

EXODUS 20:7

Somewhere along the passageways of modern church history, congregations got the idea that they had to be big. All kinds of reasons pop up: to serve the Lord better; to reach the unchurched; to furnish better programs. Whatever the reasons, to many churches, bigger seems better. And too many times, the megachurch has very nearly swallowed up the local congregation.

One troubling—or it may be amusing, depending upon one's point of view—byproduct of this rage to attract larger and larger crowds is the commercialized sermon title. Our local newspaper, for example, runs several pages of advertisements in the Saturday edition for Sunday worship services. For a few weeks I noted and jotted down sermon titles from those ads, wondering whether the titles would compel me or repel me. The list grew extensive enough to warrant categories.

Under my category "Rap Sermon Titles," I filed this one: "Have You Got a Dream? Seek Self-Esteem? Pastor Daniels on Romans 13." There we have the gospel according to *sloganese.* Another one read, "You Know No *No* in Christianity"—which sounds a bit like a spin-off on the Ten Commandments. No *no* in Christianity? The way we use words to express faith and divine mysteries says much more about who we are rather than who God is.

Years ago the American novelist William Dean Howells wrote a short story about a young lady named Editha. For Editha, to say something is to have done with it. By speaking a thing, she feels, she makes it true. She doesn't even have to pause to think. Editha finds this "gift" wonderfully handy—especially when she wants to manipulate God's will to support her designs. At one point in the story, her boyfriend refers to her theology of convenience as "pocket providence." Precisely. Editha wants to domesticate God, and pull him out of her pocket whenever she needs him. She will interpret and guide God to suit herself. Like the flimsiness of her language, the flimsiness of her theology is a deceit.

Language and theology also converge in this command-ment. The troublesome part of the commandment is the word "misuse." The King James and Revised Standard Versions translate the Hebrew as "in vain." Today's English Version puts it like this: "Do not use my name for evil purposes, for I, the Lord your God, will punish anyone who misuses my name." But what does it mean to misuse the name of the Lord, to use his name for evil purposes, or to use it "in vain"?

We may be helped by another scriptural use of the phrase "in vain" found in the book of Ecclesiastes, whose writer often refers to "vanity of vanities." A vanity is any attempt to see divine mysteries exclusively in human terms. It can't be done. Our understanding simply cannot hold God beyond his revelation of himself. Ecclesiastes 2:11 says, "Yet when I sur-veyed all that my hands had done and what I had toiled to achieve, everything was meaningless, a chasing after the wind, and there was nothing to be gained under the sun." Likewise, any attempt to humanize the divine is a vanity, an emptiness. In fact, our word "vain" derives from the Latin *vanus*: empty. When we use the name of God simply for human purposes, apart from a sense of worship and awe, we are emptying the majesty of God.

It is human vanity to think one knows everything about God; our knowledge apart from God's revelation is a com-parative emptiness. The commandment instead calls us to a worshipful awe before the mysteries of God. Modern people are often ill at ease with mysteries. We crave sure and speci-fic answers. In response to that craving, modern science, for example, is slowly filling in the gaps in our knowledge that were once simply mysteries to us. Our understanding of the human body with its intricate chemical and genetic rela-tionships has exploded many times during the last decade. With the gaps in our knowledge closing under an avalanche of technical information, we believe there must be an answer for everything.

In spiritual matters, however, there frequently is no such closure. God has not disclosed everything, but he has certainly revealed all we need to know about him. Many people are discontent with that. Even though we are called to walk by faith, not by sight, some Christians want a broad highway where they can see everything.

The longing for answers typifies human nature, for we live in an age that moves by the acquisition of knowledge—whether it be insider information on the stock market or details about tomorrow's weather. And surely we seek answers about God, by studying his word, by worshiping together, by searching out his will for us. How hard it is, then, to live with a sense of mystery, to have a calm assurance about those things we do not know, but nonetheless to testify that God knows and that suffices.

A second insight to this commandment arises as we explore what is meant by the name of God. Is there anything special about God's name that warrants this commandment?

The Meaning of God's Name

To know someone by name is the first step toward knowing that person intimately. In order to welcome someone into your acquaintance, for example, you first introduce yourself. To exchange names establishes bonds of intimacy. Likewise, a precious intimacy surrounds God's name. He has chosen to reveal himself to his chosen people, and to bring them into intimacy with him.

During the time that the Israelites were in bondage under Egyptian pharaohs, Moses spent a long time as a shepherd for his father-in-law, Jethro. It was while he was tending the sheep, as the third chapter of Exodus tells us, that he confronted a burning bush out of which God spoke to him. When Moses asked, as a sign of assurance and authority, who was speaking to him, God responded by giving this name: I Am That I Am, or Yahweh—the sacred name which

Jewish scribes represented only by consonants because the name was too holy to speak aloud.

But the point of the commandment is not to remind us of some intricate name-play. God's people are to hold him in absolute awe and reverence; yet, the remarkable thing is that God has chosen to reveal his name to his people. We might pause there a minute. What about Jesus' name? He is God, too.

About Jesus' name, we notice two things. First, Jesus bears many names and titles. We call him Immanuel because he is "God with us." We call him Christ or Messiah, because he is the anointed King of kings. And "Jesus" is the name God himself gave to his Son, through the angel Gabriel who announced the name. Jesus was not an uncommon name in the Old Testament. Joshua, Jehoshua, and other names are forms of it. But all these mean the same thing: "God is our salvation." By naming his own son "Jesus," God shows that *here*, in the flesh, is our salvation.

This second thing about Jesus' name hearkens back to the sacred title by which God revealed himself to Moses: *I Am That I Am*. God is creator and absolute Lord—the essential being. He is the great *I Am*, through whom and only through whom we have eternal life. In his conversation with a group of followers, Jesus identifies himself by the same sacred name that God used to Moses. Jesus says, "I tell you the truth. Before Abraham was born, I am!" (John 8:58). Jesus declares himself to be one with the great Creator Lord.

In this commandment, we become aware of the precious, holy intimacy by which God has chosen to reveal himself through his name to his people. God's name is holy, for the name evokes God himself. Scripture resounds with the majesty of God's name. In the Psalms, David writes, "O Lord, our Lord, how majestic is thy name in all the earth" (8:1). People are to use that majestic name only in reverence and in holy worship. When we know God so intimately as to speak with him by name, we are no longer distant strangers. We are close friends. Matters of the heart can be laid open. We walk together in our daily living, not as travelers in opposite directions but as friends going hand in hand. This intimate relationship is the blessing that accompanies knowing and properly using the name of God.

Now comes the hard part. What does it mean to use that name *in vain?*

1. Swearing

The most obvious example of using God's name in vain is to use it in swearing or cursing. All such usage drags God's name down through the mud of human emotions. It subjects the Almighty Lord to one's emotional impulses. Mindless use of God's name is wrong because it reduces God himself in our minds and to those who hear us.

People may not think of it that way when they swear. In fact, swearing seems for many people simply a habit or a pattern of speech. One doesn't have far to look for examples of a verbal assault upon God's name. Street conversation ripples with expletives that call out God's name, and some of the music blasting out of passing cars thunders a defiance of his holy name that can be heard a block away.

Dangerous misuse of God's name has become almost casual in modern society. For a time, movies seemed riddled with a profaning of God's name, but now the blasphemy has inundated all the popular media. Many books treat God's name with a flippancy that is saddening; even the most popular television programs feature dialogue that is punctuated by frequent swearing in God's name. It was not so long ago that one could avoid such language simply by avoiding the sources. Now it seems we are surrounded with profanity as unavoidable as breathing. What is made commonplace in such profanity is the majesty of God. The sense of sacredness, of holy awe, is lost from our lives when we reduce all to a low level in our thought and speech. The tender, loving relationship with the Holy God is damaged when his name is called out in mindless and even cruel invectives.

JACKSWANN

2. Reflex Religion

A second vain use of God's name is reflected in some sermon slogans one reads in the "catchy" newspaper advertisements for worship services: "Have You Got a Dream? Seek Self-Esteem? Pastor Daniels on Romans 13." It's what I call "reflex religion."

It works like this. Whenever someone gets in trouble they suddenly call out to God to help them. If they get out of their trouble, they forget all about God. This kind of religion is illustrated by a prayer one coach used before soccer games in high school. The team would gather around, and he would mumble something like "Help us play well to your glory. Amen." Then the players would holler, "Kill 'em!" It's like the magical religions that we considered in chapter 1.

People who participate in reflex religion have no true relationship with God. Things happen that terrify or worry them, and they don't know where to go or what to do. Suddenly they heave out prayers like desperate half-court basketball shots, hoping they'll get lucky and hit the hoop with one. Sure can't hurt to try it, they figure. The tragic thing is that it's not only people without religious commitment who practice such reflexive use of God's name; some people within the church do also. For them, too, God's name is to be mouthed only in the hour of need. Now this is not necessarily all bad. In fact it can well be the beginning point of something more, maybe even the very first steps into a close relationship with God. Reflex religion does, after all, acknowledge one's need and looks for a way out.

Each commandment may be understood in a negative and a positive way. For example, the first commandment tells us that we should have no other gods before the Lord God. But it also tells us, by implication, the blessings that come to us when we worship God with all our heart and soul and mind and strength. In a similar way, this commandment has a positive counterpart as well. In her book *Smoke on the Mountain*, Joy Davidman (the wife of C. S. Lewis) writes that a necessary corollary to this commandment must be, "Thou shalt take the name of the Lord our God in earnest." By that she meant a holy, grateful, awe-filled reverence that permeates our words and our actions—that turns our very life into an act of constant worship.

If swearing and reflex religion are two obvious examples of using God's name in vain, a third example is a bit more ambiguous—but it may be even more pertinent to the daily life of Christians. It is possible for Christians who would not dream of swearing, and whose spiritual lives have grown far beyond mere reflex religion, to still to be held accountable to this commandment. Some Christians simply use God's name too loosely.

3. Frivolous Use of God's Name

Loose or frivolous use of the Lord's name is also a violation of the commandment. Such talk can arise from the lips of even the most sincere Christians. It appears in many ways: "My Lord!" as an exclamation, or "Oh, my God" as an expression of surprise. The God Almighty, Creator of heaven and earth, is used as little more than a punctuation mark of human speech.

God is not to be taken casually. He doesn't permit that. Truly Jesus came as God with us, in human flesh. And truly he has become our intimate friend. But at what cost! The cost of confrontation with hell itself on the cross—for us and in our place. In that context, this casual use of God's name, this sort of friendly glibness, is a use of God's name in vain. If people use his name as lightly as a breath, they have forgotten the majesty of God who gave them breath and the suffering of Christ who redeemed the breather.

Remember the two Israelite pilgrims, Joel and Rachel, whom we considered in the preface? They approached the tabernacle with fear and trembling; they stood before the Holy of Holies with awe and terror—here was the very presence of God.

We also stand before the presence of God when we call his name. The name invokes the being; it brings us into the Holy of Holies. "You may ask me for anything in my name," Jesus said, "and I will do it" (John 14:14). This is the name at which every knee will bow and every tongue confess the Lordship of Christ. It bears every bit of the sacredness of the Holy of Holies.

We see, then, three instances of using God's name in vain. But we still must explore the heart of this commandment. The essence of this law is not simply a negative proscription, but a positive prescription. Using something in vain, after all, is a violation of a positive action, and the positive core of this commandment has to do with loyalty. Fundamentally, if one takes God's name in vain, one's heart is not set firmly in allegiance to God.

Loyalty

The relationship at the heart of this commandment is not unlike the vows made between knights and a king during the Middle Ages. According to legend, King Arthur had a vision of an empire at peace, ruled in accord with God's will. He wanted to drive back the "beast of darkness," or the anarchy that plagued early Britain. Unable to do this by himself, he called certain knights to the service of this ideal, thus forming the Round Table.

When these knights joined the Table, they swore allegiance to Arthur and to his vision. The medieval term for that relationship was *liege*, which means allegiance or loyalty. The knights took vows of faithfulness, honorable deeds, generosity, and courtly manners.

The Sovereign God also has called his people to allegiance, to fidelity. We are bound in *liege* to God. The blessing of this is that, as with Arthur and his knights, our king is on our side as we are on his. He is faithful to help us from his position of majesty. We can know that we are not alone in our Christian living.

What God has fashioned with his believers, however, is something much more powerful than the knightly vows of the Middle Ages. Indeed, it is a covenant, and one of a very special kind. It may be illuminated by understanding covenants during Old Testament times in general. The Old Testament covenant was a pact between a sovereign lord and his subjects. Only the sovereign had the right to initiate the treaty. There was no collective bargaining, no union at work here. All things belonged to the ruler. The sovereign had the authority to extend the treaty, and he did so only because of his concern or love for the people. What he asked for in return was loyalty. He stipulated certain blessings if the treaty was kept, and certain curses if the people broke fidelity.

The Ten Commandments are, of course, a covenant, and one that follows the pattern of such treaties. God calls to us his people. He tells us how to live in a blessed relationship with him. But he also asks for our loyalty. He asks for our choice, our wholehearted devotion to following his commandments. But it does seem, doesn't it, that so often we fail. We're tempted to cut corners off certain commandments. We want to negotiate others. We look for allegiances and alliances in all the wrong places.

Let me tell you about one of my experiences with human loyalties and the truth that I learned from it. I call it "The Lesson of the Christmas Card."

I can remember my thoughts as I stood with her Christmas card in my hand, ready to tape it to the door frame of the living room. This card she sent me was like several dozen other Christmas cards I have hung on the door frame according to the custom of three generations in our family.

"That way we walk through the doorways with our friends," my mother often said. She smiled when she said it, remembering. Her mother had said it before her.

The card she sent me was like so many others, but it held me longer. I suddenly saw the smile in the words penned across the bottom: *We have a daughter. She is my pride and joy.*

Those words wrenched loose tears pent up too long. Not just another card; this was a life I held in my hand. My thoughts drifted back to a time years earlier . . .

Her young face haunted me—eyes like wide, hurt pools of bereavement, empty of joy and laughter, the skin of her cheeks pallid under the street lamp. She had telephoned me, but had been unable to talk. First there was only a thick silence, then the choking gasp of her sobs as she tried to talk.

"Stay where you are," I told her. "I'll be there in a minute."

And so I went out to where she stood forlornly in the light of a street lamp by a telephone booth. And I went thinking these things.

What right had she to demand my time? She was but one of two-hundred and twelve students I had that semester. Over two-hundred students! I didn't even know all their names.

"I hurt," she said.

"Tell me," I said, and a voice in the back of my brain screamed *Time. Four lectures tomorrow. Two-hundred and twelve students.*

"I had these pills in my hand when I called," she said.

"Give me the pills," I said. I held out my hand, fearful that she would run. But she handed them over in the small brown vial. I caught the hand. I looked at it. Twigs laced together by blue veins under a tissue of skin.

And then I saw the burns on the backs of her wrists. Small circular holes in the skin like stab wounds.

"Cigarettes?" I asked.

The small voice was a hiss in the night. "I hate myself."

"Let's walk," I said. "It's easier to talk that way."

The words came slowly and thick with fear at first, as if her tongue were hypnotized by pain: "My father died. I don't have a father. I want a father."

Why me? I can't be your father, child, I thought. *Friend, maybe. Or helper. Or "counselor"—that fine, safe, professional word. But not father.*

She had no father. I had too many students—plus a real family of my own. We talked, she and I. For days thereafter we talked and talked. I kept the pills in my desk and later discarded them. Some of the burns healed. But not the pain. And then she started to stay away.

When my wife and I came home one Friday night from the college Christmas concert, it had been raining hard. We came home late. The baby-sitter met us at the door.

"She said it would be all right," the sitter said nervously. "Said she knew you. Said . . ."

"Who?"

The baby-sitter pointed.

She cringed on the floor alongside the sofa, water dripping from the tangled, matted hair, the blue sweatshirt soggy with rain, the harsh, choking sobs wracking her throat.

My wife cleaned her and dried her and made a bed for her on the cot in the study where I would have to grade papers the next day. And I sat alone by the damp puddle she had left near the sofa. I was only eight years older than she! Not old enough to be her father. So I fumbled for excuses.

She was still sleeping the next morning, without drugs for the first time in a long time, and maybe because of that. I said good morning and she didn't answer. Her thin shape lay under the blankets, like a battered doll. Understand, I had to grade those papers. I sat at the desk looking past the pools of ink that shifted under my eyes.

Over the Christmas holidays she didn't want to go home. There was no home, she said. A mother whom she thought hated her. A father dead. No one to care for her, to love her. That's all right, we agreed, she can stay here.

My two children, who *could* call me father, were therapy of a rambunctious, unpatterned kind. She rolled with them on the floor. She wanted to be one of them. I know this now.

But the time came when we had to take her to a clinic, once a week. Then to the psychiatric ward of a hospital fifty miles away, for a longer stay—we didn't know how long.

What could I do? Love I could give, not healing.

The practical concerns of admissions forms and insurance papers finally involved her mother. And we returned to our own tasks, our lives, carrying an empty space in our hearts.

In time, distance grew between us. And, in time, the questions that had haunted me found answers. It was Christmas when she first came to be with us. It was Christmas when she returned to us through this card. I *was* a father to this child, despite my clumsy efforts to shirk the role. In my own fumbling way, I loved her as my child.

And now I reached for the Scotch tape. Mother said that our friends watch us through the doorway of their cards. So I press her card to the frame.

And I see myself kneeling by her side next to that old cot.

And I see her husband by the side of his wife and their daughter. O my child, I love you.

Here is the difference between our human allegiances and God's allegiance. Too often our own allegiances prove frail and weak. Despite our best intentions, we constantly stumble over our own humanity. But not God. His faithfulness is new every morning. He kneels by the cot of our sorrow and pain and holds our hand. That very fact demonstrates the beauty, the breathtaking majesty of this commandment. God's allegiance never fails. We are told here to honor his name, not because it is the name of just any ruler, but because it is the name of the only Just Ruler. It names God Almighty, maker of heaven and earth, who has vowed never to leave us nor forsake us.

REFLECTIONS

1. How does the language we use, the words we choose, reveal who we are? How do our words reflect our beliefs about God?

   How can our choice of words affect our prayers and the results of those prayers?

2. This commandment is about proper use of God's name. Think for a moment about the various names for God that you have heard and that you have used. Which names are most meaningful to you?

   How does the name you use for God affect the way you think about God?

3. The chapter lists several ways in which one can "take the name of the Lord in vain," or "misuse" God's name. Can you think of additional examples?

4. Many religious groups (churches and organizations) try to attract new members by advertising. Recall examples you have seen of such advertising. How effective were they? How honest or truthful were they?

   How legitimate is such advertising as a means of evangelism?

5. Under the heading entitled **The Meaning of God's Name,** the author writes "God's name is holy, for the name evokes God himself." What does this mean, or how is it true?

How does that thought make you feel? How might its truth affect your prayers? Your daily speech? Your use of all language?

6. In biblical times, the name of God was considered so sacred and fearful that it was never spoken: Jewish scribes represented the sacred name only by consonants. As this chapter points out, times and attitudes have changed. Do you see the change in attitudes as good or bad?

What is lost from our lives when we use God's name in sinful, thoughtless, or casual ways? How is our relationship with God damaged?

4

Finding Rest in God

Remember the Sabbath day by keeping it holy.
Six days you shall labor and do all your work,
but the seventh day is a Sabbath
to the Lord your God.
On it you shall not do any work, neither you,
nor your son or daughter,
nor your manservant or maidservant,
nor your animals, nor the alien within your gates.
For in six days the Lord made the heavens and the
earth, the sea, and all that is in them,
but he rested on the seventh day.
Therefore the Lord blessed the Sabbath day
and made it holy.

EXODUS 20:8-11

For some reason that I did not understand when I was young, every other month or so my parents packed us kids into the old Ford on a Sunday morning, and we drove to attend services at one of two inner-city gospel churches. The one I can't forget is the True Light Church. It stood tucked back on one of the most decayed streets of our city.

True Light Church was a four-square little church, clapboard sides peeling white paint, a virtually indistinguishable sign nailed above the door. The pews were old, worn down to the bare wood. The floors were planks. In the front two rows were seated the twelve elders of the congregation. We often sat in the third row, our white faces the only ones in that church.

The pulpit stood, what seemed to my young eyes, very high above us on a platform, next to which was a baptismal font. The rhythms of the music, the very loud call and response of the choir, still seem to move in me. The large, beautiful voice of Reverend Patterson speaking the Word still echoes in my hearing.

Although we were the only white faces, I never felt like an outsider at that church. It seemed a second home. In fact, when I entered college in the Sixties and began seeking my own church home, I often went to that church with a few friends. The services were long, usually two hours or more. The streets were, if anything, meaner than I'd remembered them from my childhood visits, the building even shabbier.

So it was that I was there on the night Reverend Patterson baptized his son, a handsome young man about my own age. He moved with a fine athletic grace, proud and poised, up to the pulpit to stand beside his father. Reverend Patterson led his son to the baptismal font. I was now more than tall enough to see that there were steps descending into the font. When they climbed down, the water overflowed and trickled across the pulpit area.

The people sang, in a low hum at first as they found the familiar notes of the melody; then they let the song flow freely. As the volume of the song rose, so did the elders. All twelve of them stood as one body. They walked up the steps to the baptismal font; then, one by one, the song now a strong outpouring of love from their throats, they climbed down into the baptismal font. And the flow of water, which had been a trickle, now became a wave, washing down over the sides, moving across the floor in streams, washing around my own feet. It was like grace, poured out and overflowing at a moment when the Holy Spirit, too, came down and washed through that place.

In my lifetime I have worshiped in many churches in many different places, from dusty little buildings in the rural South to vaulted cathedrals in eastern cities and in Europe. I will never forget that night at True Light Church. And for good reason.

A few years later, after I had started graduate school and then had to leave for service in the military, I received news of True Light Church. It had grown during the last few years and had moved to a new location. But it had lost one member. Reverend Patterson's son, baptized that night some years before, had been killed in action in Vietnam. True Light Church was commemorating his death and his life eternal. I couldn't attend the service because I was in Vietnam myself, stationed not far from where Reverend Patterson's son was killed. I have not been to that particular church in the years since. Yet it is forever a part of me, and I am forever grateful for that worship, and for the times I kept the Sabbath with members of True Light.

I think of those times now because this commandment on Sabbath keeping seems so intimately connected in our minds with traditions and ways of worship.

Supposedly, this is the commandment that every minister loves—and perhaps grieves over. How much does Sabbath observance apply in these whirlwind days of modern life? How much is Sabbath observance simply a matter of tradition? Or, does the commandment itself govern traditions? Religious, family, and denominational traditions seem tied up with this commandment in a way shared by none of the other nine.

Some of us can recall in our own family traditions a host of restrictions on what we could or could not do on Sunday. My own family was not exempt. My mother, for example, peeled all the vegetables for the Sunday meal on Saturday night. She had them all sitting on the stove in pots, so that all she had to do on Sunday was turn on the gas.

No work on Sunday.

Some of my friends had "no work on Sunday" extended to "no fun on Sunday." For example, the family of my closest friend rented a cottage for three weeks during the summer. On Sunday he could put on his swimming suit, but he couldn't go in the water. He could take a boat ride, but it had to be very, very slow. He could ride his bicycle, but not out of the driveway. He'd ride in a little circle until he was so dizzy he couldn't see straight. Other friends of mine could listen to the radio, but only softly. And no rock and roll.

No fun on Sunday.

As I look around my own religiously polyglot neighborhood today, I observe a host of different practices. One neighboring family goes to church on Sunday morning, and then straight to a restaurant and from there out to the beach or a bowling alley. Down the block is another family that, should they run out of milk on a Sunday, would not think of going to the store to buy more. They will do without milk. A bit farther down the street is a family that mows the lawn, washes the cars, and attends to all other such chores on Sunday.

One family's Sunday traditions are offset by those of another family. Lifestyles conflict like steel balls in a game of Crossfire. But it has been that way throughout history. This is not solely a contemporary issue.

Step back a moment to Jesus' day and look again at his chief tormentors—some of the self-righteous Pharisees and their law-abiding brethren. In those days, Pharisees were considered the social scions, kings of righteousness, pillars of propriety and rectitude. And some, indeed, strove to live God-pleasing lives. But others became caught up in an empty, outward show of piety, constantly alert to countless human and often trivial laws, while their hearts were filled with pride and self-satisfaction.

Nowhere did these great legalists clash more dramatically with Jesus than on the issue of Sabbath observance, for here the Pharisees really relished their rules. In fact, they had hundreds of rules for keeping the Sabbath "holy." That legalism incited more than one conflict with Jesus. We remember, for example, the time some Pharisees chastised Jesus for picking grain on the Sabbath in order to satisfy the disciples' hunger. Here, and in a later instance when he healed on the Sabbath, Jesus responded to human needs with acts of mercy. The original Sabbath, instituted by God, was very much of the same order: a day set aside after creation for rest. The commandment to observe this day of rest was also an act of mercy by a benevolent God who seeks relationships rather than rules. We need time, we need quiet and reflection, to establish our relationship with God. God says, in effect, I am available to you. I want to spend time with you.

But move up in history a good many years, closer to our own time and experience. Ride, for a moment, with those few noble souls, the Puritans, as they traveled to the shores of our nation in the early seventeenth century. There is much to admire about these people. Their courage was breathtaking, their fortitude unbending, their convictions unyielding. An admirable people, and one intent upon establishing a Christian nation. There is much to appreciate in the Puritans; but as one looks more closely at their lives and temperament, another side surfaces.

Few other traditions ever provided a greater list of "shalt

nots" for Sabbath observance than the American Puritans. The Puritans considered themselves a chosen nation, a people set apart. Their colony was, in their words, "God's American Israel." And they had strict rules for Sabbath observance. No cooking. No church decorations (they called church the "meeting house"). No travel. No kissing or whistling. In fact, they even imposed a fine on married people who had sexual intercourse on the Sabbath. They arrived at a determination for this last offense in a most ingenious way. If a child was born on the Sabbath, they believed that the child was conceived on the Sabbath—an automatic fine. So if a woman started going into labor on Saturday night, she had some fast and furious work to do to meet the deadline.

A pattern emerges in these proscriptive traditions. Somehow humans still feel the obligation of carrying a large sack of "shalt nots" across their backs in order to earn God's grace. The result, all too often, is a pinched and austere religious spirit very much like the Puritans or the Pharisees. While we recognize that rules can be (and most often are) good things, we must also realize that rules can become ends in themselves. And this is dangerous ground.

What makes the territory dangerous is the fact that traditions and rituals are important to us as believers. They hone our faith. They help us integrate belief into daily living. Traditions are precious: they form the book of memories we pore over the rest of our lives. However, while affirming our precious traditions, we can also understand the hollowness of rules merely for the sake of rules.

Observance of the Sabbath is not to be equated solely with human traditions or rituals. Traditions change as humanity changes. What we practiced yesterday, we practice differently today, and might not practice at all tomorrow. What is the enduring message of this commandment, transcending all human rules and rituals? How do we honor God's commandment to keep the Sabbath holy and yet avoid a pietistic legalism that puts human rules in place of God? If we understand rightly the freedom that we have in Christ, perhaps we can discover some creative ways to keep the Sabbath in our modern culture.

Sabbath as Freedom From?

Jesus' response to the Pharisees about Sabbath observance may be seen as part of his concept of freedom. On the one hand, Jesus clearly supports the commandments that God instituted ("'It is easier for heaven and earth to disappear than for the least stroke of a pen to drop out of the Law'" Luke 16:17), but on the other hand Jesus scorns law keeping that disregards the spirit of love behind the law. The reason should be clear: Jesus sees the law as a means to a loving relationship with God, not as a tool to make someone feel small and distant from God. This is particularly important to keep in mind as we see what this commandment has freed us for.

Sabbath as Freedom For . . .

If, as Jesus says in John 8:32, we are freed in him, then we are freed from a system of legalistic, human-centered living that strives to earn God's love by our own merit. We are freed from bondage. But we are also *freed for* a certain kind of living. True freedom, we are reminded, has both direction and a goal: the direction comes from the divine authority of God with guidance for our Christian living, and the goal is a right relationship with God. Here the meaning of Sabbath and the way we observe it achieve greater clarity.

The first step in that direction arises from the very word *Sabbath*, a word we seldom use anymore. We often now worship on Sunday, to signal Jesus' resurrection on the first day of the week—the joyful day, the day of liberation. Only when we remember that the word *Sabbath* means "rest," however, can we begin to understand fully how we are free to enjoy a resting in God's grace.

Sabbath as Rest

When God instituted a Sabbath rest, it was not simply for himself. Obviously, God has no need of a physical rest. Rather, the Sabbath is ordained as an act of mercy for God's creation, a period set aside for relaxation, for fellowship, and for rejoicing in this good world God has made; and for communing with, or worshiping, this good God. The Sabbath rest thereby was part of God's created order. Even though Christians changed their day of worship to Sunday, the principle of the Sabbath commandment did not change.

We stand in need psychologically, spiritually, and physically, of a rest from our labor. We need to set time aside for God, to refresh ourselves and our relationship with God— a relationship that can suffer under our normal workload. But we also need, like first-century Christians, to worship together in community. Perhaps it does not matter exactly how long or how often one worships, but we can safely say that it has to be a regular, frequent part of the Christian life.

The pattern of the commandments given thus far is revealing. They are not merely a list of rules, but an orderly, thematically unified covenant telling us how to live in love with our Lord. First, God announces his holiness and his love. He forbids idolatry. He forbids misuse of his name because he is holy. And now he tells us how to worship him: in holiness and truth, not in a host of "shalt nots," not in fear or empty tradition. This commandment should not be understood as what God forbids, but as what God offers in our spirit of Christian freedom: holy worship.

The Sabbath commandment is an invitation, a blessing or privilege, to worship God. But it is also a requirement if we wish to grow strong in a loving relationship with God. Because God knows what is best for us, we can't view the commandment simply as an option. It is a requirement for spiritual well-being. That requirement is enforced elsewhere in Scripture in direct and emphatic terms. In a passage on the folly of human rituals for worshiping God, the Old Testament prophet Isaiah directs the Israelites to first things. In Isaiah 58:13-14, he says:

If you keep your feet from breaking the Sabbath
and from doing as you please on my holy day,
if you call the Sabbath a delight
and the Lord's holy day honorable,
and if you honor it by not going your own way
and not doing as you please or speaking idle words,
then you will find your joy in the Lord,
and I will cause you to ride on the heights of the land
and to feast on the inheritance of your father Jacob.

This injunction, Isaiah emphatically points out, is from the "mouth of the Lord" himself. Isaiah's call echoes into the New Testament. John tells us how the disciples gathered on the first day of the week and how the resurrected Jesus himself came and stood among them, saying, "Peace be with you," as a benediction upon their gathering. Acts 20:7 tells us that "On the first day of the week, when we were gathered together to break bread, Paul talked with them, intending to depart on the morrow; and he prolonged his speech until midnight." That sounds a great deal like the exposition of the word, the central event of any worship service. The purpose of worship, in addition to human fellowship, is to commune with God by examining his will as revealed in Scripture. Hebrews 10:23-25, moreover, encourages us to

not give up meeting together, as some are in the habit of
doing, but let us encourage one another—and all the more as
you see the Day approaching.

The pattern of worship shapes a regular part of the believer's life. During times of worship, Jesus says, he is with us: "For where two or three come together in my name, there I am with them" (Matthew 18:20). That worship can occur in any context, in the sparkling sprawl of the megachurch, or in the storefront cubbyhole. Where people gather in Christ's name, he is in the midst of them.

Creative Freedom

In Romans 14:5-7, Paul writes:

One man esteems one day as better than another, while another man esteems all days alike. Let every one be fully convinced in his own mind. He who observes the day, observes it in honor of the Lord.

His point is cautionary, but also permits us to see this commandment as a means of grace, as a way to strengthen our loving relationship with God. We draw close to God in worship so that he may draw close to us. The commandment tells us that "The Lord blessed the Sabbath day and made it holy"; the very blessing and holiness of it lies in God's presence with us as we worship him.

Our aim in worship is to behold God. Applying the commandment to our busy lives, however, can be as tricky as navigating through a thicket of thornbushes. Several suggestions might make the passage easier and more fruitful for Christians in a modern culture. These arise not just from my own experience with worship, but from a lifetime of observing what works for others and trying to apply their lessons to my own family.

My wife, Pat, and I are perhaps a bit peculiar in this matter of worship. For one thing, we have often had to adapt our worship to the churches and denominations in geographical areas we have lived—in the Deep South, in the foothills of the Appalachians, in Pennsylvania, in New York, now in Michigan. We have been members of several different denominations, have attended worship services of nearly every Christian denomination, have worshiped in styles ranging from pulse-pounding praise-fests to polished and traditional liturgies.

One constant remains. We prepare our hearts before worship. Sunday observance does not begin on Sunday morning. It begins earlier in the week by prayer for ourselves, our children, and our church. I can't remember a Saturday when we haven't prayed over Sunday, a prayer of submission, expectation, and blessing. I can practically guarantee, for myself at least, that without this preparation, Sunday worship comes as a sort of harried intrusion rather than a hallowed intercession.

A second technique helps us. We try to shape our traditions to the day, rather than the day to the traditions. If we want festivity; we plan it. This often takes work. If we want family togetherness, we make time for it, and often for a fine meal that unifies that time. But we also leave time and freedom for experimentation. If God gives us a day that is splendid in beauty, it would seem to us something of a crime not to enjoy it by taking a hike, or driving to a park or lake to relax and appreciate the gift.

We make efforts to help our children have a meaningful time of worship. This can be done in church services, and it can be done after they are over. Dozens of top-notch children's devotionals and worship materials are available. Instead of sitting glued to some televised sports event, try watching a good Christian video together, or sing along with favorite hymns or gospel songs on tape.

We also have "special" family traditions. Most Sundays we—even the grown and married children—gather for dinner. Children bring friends if they want. Sometimes the meal is quite elaborate; sometimes it's grilled outside. Often we break out old trays of slides or photo albums. The main joy, however, is just being together as people who love the Lord. These traditions may enrich our relations with others in our family, but they are ultimately directed toward the entire family's relationship with God. Herein, and I would say herein alone, lies the hallowedness of Sunday—the opportunity to renew or deepen our relationship with the God who yearns to meet us in love.

REFLECTIONS

1. Think back over the Sundays in your life. Are these good memories or not-so-good memories? What positive highlights stand out? What, if anything, made Sunday a special day for you?

   How do Sundays affect your life of faith?

   Most calendars list Sunday as the first day of a new week. People often think of Sunday as the last day of a weekend. Which understanding of Sunday is most meaningful to you? Which understanding seems better suited to the commandment's instruction to "Remember the Sabbath day by keeping it holy"?

2. How do you define "worship"?

   What is most meaningful to you about your Sunday worship? About the church service—the building itself, the music, the sermon, the readings, or the people who surround you during this time?

   What do you get out of your worship service?

   How could your service be made even better? How could *you* make the service better?

   What could you do to make Sunday more meaningful?

3. The opening pages of this chapter describe the author's childhood experiences worshiping at the True Light Church. According to the author, what made those worship experiences so memorable? What else do you think contributed to his positive memories of those church services?

4. The observance of Sabbath—a day of rest—has its roots in the very beginnings of our world. God paused after creating the earth to take a day of rest. How is *our* observance of the Sabbath also a part of God's creation? How does it focus our sights on the Creator God and his creation?

What does this understanding of "Sabbath" say about rules and traditions and the spirit of our worship?

5. The Old Testament book of Isaiah contains a beautiful promise for those who keep God's day holy:

If you keep your feet from breaking the Sabbath and from doing what you please on my holy day, if you call the Sabbath a delight and the Lord's holy day honorable, and if you honor it by not going your own way and not doing as you please or speaking idle words, then you will find your joy in the Lord, and I will cause you to ride on the heights of the land and to feast on the inheritance of your father Jacob.

The key part of this promise is "you will find your joy in the Lord." How does this sum up the entire spirit behind this commandment? What are the blessings that *you* have discovered from "finding your joy in the Lord"?

6. The final section of this chapter suggests several techniques that can help make Sundays "special." These have become, for the author, traditions handed down to his family. Think of two Sunday "traditions" that you practice or that you could start—ways of passing on Sunday joy to your family or friends.

5

Putting Relationships in Order

Honor your father and your mother,

so that you may live long in the land

the Lord your God is giving you.

EXODUS 20:12

The buildings along upper Division Avenue in Grand Rapids, Michigan, are decayed with time and abuse. Windows are boarded up, doors hang askew, the red brick is crumbling and dirty. The wind funnels through the rows of buildings, blowing litter along the asphalt of Division Avenue. Rusted hulks of automobiles litter the side streets. This is the kind of neighborhood where motorists lock their car doors.

A few blocks over from Division, the great snarl of expressways serving downtown Grand Rapids curl and thread above, around, and below each other. They channel thousands of automobiles a day to the shiny, glass-plated office buildings several blocks north. A few motorists still take Division Avenue, perhaps to avoid the rush of the expressways.

On one corner, where Weston Street angles downhill through potholes and crosses Division, a section of one ruined building has been reclaimed. Passing by in a car, one would hardly notice it's there—a doorfront and a plate glass window, one of the few not barred or boarded over. The sign on the door reads "Heartside Clinic." Few people know about the place, only the ones who need it—the homeless wanderers of Division Avenue. Those bereft of family, of parents and children. Those who sleep in the missions or under the bridges of the expressways.

For several years now, that clinic has been a second home to my wife, Pat, who volunteers there as a nurse. It is the first home to the wanderers of Division Avenue. Sponsored by a local hospital, staffed in large part by volunteer doctors, nurses, and social workers, Heartside Clinic is a place where people care.

As part of the procedures at the Heartside Clinic, staffers have to take down a medical history for each patient, one item of which asks for an address. Answers vary. Some people list a nearby mission. Some list an orchard where they last worked with migrant field hands. One listed the expressway overpass, under which a cardboard-box shantytown has arisen. These are the homeless who come to Heartside.

The stories of their family pasts are tales of nearly unrelenting tragedy. Whether because of abuse, or criminal records, or histories of mental illness, many of these people are virtually severed from family pasts. They are truly homeless—without a place to call "home" and, even more tragically, without family to give meaning to a home. The reality of their situation is almost too cruel to comprehend.

"Honor your father and your mother." How does this commandment speak to people such as those at the Heartside Clinic? And how does it speak to countless numbers of us who, in our own ways, are also struggling to find a sense of home and family in our lives? These are questions that need exploring. But first it will be helpful to look at the context of the commandment and the concepts that underlie it.

The Pattern of Authority

This commandment introduces a transition in the pattern of God's laws. In fact, theologians speak of two "tables" of the law. The first table includes those laws that tell us how to worship God, while the second table includes laws that tell us how to live with others as children of God. This commandment introduces the second table by telling us how to live with others, but particularly with our parents. The *why* behind the commandment rests in the first table: the authority of God and our relationship with him.

In a Christian home, parents represent an authority structure to the children, which is different from merely representing rules or rule givers. One might see God as a God of rules or as a God of authority—two quite different things, and ones that depend upon our perspective. Those who willingly obey the rules will do so because they recognize the authority. Those who fail to recognize the authority will see only rules.

This commandment, which Martin Luther called the "first and greatest" of the second table, might *seem* to tell us simply to obey the *rules* of the parents. But it doesn't say that. It tells us to honor our parents, to recognize their place of authority over us. In God's pattern, parents represent an intermediary human structure between God's authority and our obedient responsibility. We are obedient and responsible to the authority of parents who are obedient and responsible to the authority of God.

The commandment raises two further questions: What is the responsibility of parents who represent God's authority to their children? And what is the responsibility of children to such parents? In short, what does it mean to "honor" honorable parents?

The Commandment with Promise

It is important in this age when traditional family structures seem to be crumbling to see the specialness, the Scripture-wide support of this commandment. The family is God's first and foremost social structure. It is his divine instrument, and this commandment, here on the divide between two tables, lies at the very heart of it. So important is it that God attaches a promise to it. Do this, God says, "That your days may be long in the land which the Lord your God gives you."

When God gave the commandment, the Israelites had no land. They were literally homeless, wandering in the wilderness during their exile. God had promised that he would give them a land, and the foundation of that homeland, as well as their society, would be the family structure under God. That family structure, which lies at the heart of this commandment, offered everything—protection, nourishment, love, and a host of other necessities for survival and life.

Consider a bit further the significance of this tremendous promise. It promises a homeland—at the very moment when the people had no land. It promises them a safe place. But a land means little, and it surely is not a homeland, without a people to home it. The truly dramatic part of this promise for any Israelite was how the promise from the eternal God extends to future generations. Sons and daughters, and their children from generation to generation, will have a safe place, a homeland. The order of God's society grows out of the home where God comes first and parents enact his authority.

Such implications also introduce an awesome responsibility for us who are part of those "future generations." Parents stand in the place of God in the family, and their children are to honor them as God's representatives. Here is the ideal structure established by God for his family of believers.

The publishing presses of the United States, both Christian and secular, have poured out hundreds of books that give guidance for "successful parenting." They speak to the desperate need families have for direction in an age that has diminished and even demeaned the traditional family. I suppose there may be some "perfect families" out there—their lives all in order, physically, socially, and spiritually. Their children exhaust themselves in obedience, seldom disobey, thank their parents for disciplining them when the tiniest infraction occurs, and are all in line to become neurosurgeons, evangelists, or trial attorneys. My family isn't like that. I'm not sure what professions my children will choose, for example. The only hope I have is that they will be led by God to follow his will in whatever they do. I don't know whom they will marry, and I bite my tongue to keep from giving suggestions. The only guideline I give in that matter is that the person loves the Lord with all his or her heart. Anything beyond that is open.

I have frankly needed, and still need, all the help I can get in fulfilling my responsibility as a parent. Yet, there seem to be so very few really good directions that apply to my—*our*—family. Each individual family is unique; no one set of specifics suits all. It is a desperate and confusing time for the American family.

Scripture does provide some worthy specifics. The Old Testament book of Proverbs, for example, is sometimes called the "Book on Family Life." In a passage like Proverbs 4:1, we read "Listen, my sons, to a father's instruction, pay attention and gain understanding." Or, again, Proverbs 23:22-25, "Hearken to your father who begot you, and do not despise your mother when she is old. Buy truth, and do not sell it; buy wisdom, instruction, and understanding. The father of the righteous will greatly rejoice; he who begets a wise son will be glad in him. Let your father and mother be glad, let her who bore you rejoice." Here God gives specific instructions in how we are to honor our parents. We are to heed their instructions. We are to care for them when they are old. We are to honor them by being honest and wise, choosing the right thing.

The commandment to honor our parents also receives support in the New Testament. Jesus himself repeated its words, as recorded in Matthew 15:4. And, in chapter 6 of his letter to the Ephesians, Paul repeats the commandment as part of his advice on how Christians are to live in the world, and his description of authority structures in the Christian's life.

When one considers these admonitions carefully, however, one may feel bewildered by the very lack of specificity in them. Not one tells us how to deal with a daughter diagnosed with attention-deficit disorder. Not one tells us how to confront a daughter who ignores her curfew, who creeps into the house with her clothing in disarray, and who responds with defiance to her parents' pleas. Not one specifically addresses the son experimenting with marijuana during the high school lunch hour. Nor do they address, in specific terms, any of the host of temptations that bedevil young persons today.

Indeed, the advice that is presented is often scorned or simply dismissed by some in our culture as relics of a primitive past; these Bible verses have no more to tell us, some say, than the hieroglyphs found on some ancient mausoleum. They are "impractical."

If one is looking for specifics suited to each individual behavioral issue, of course Scripture will not meet the expectation. However, it does something much better than providing an encyclopedia of child care. It deals with principles and values that guide all our practical decisions. Scripture is not some time-bound book of rules; rather, it establishes the authority structure that governs our hearts. Nowhere is this more pertinent than in this particular commandment.

This commandment charges parents with responsibility to enact God's authority in a way that will warrant their children's honor—to be *honorable* parents; and it charges children to respond to those parents by honoring them. Implicit in the commandment is the assumption that parents are representing authority honorably. If we can establish the tasks of such parents, we may better understand the responsibility of their children.

The Tasks of Honorable Parents

1. To Love
The first task of honorable parents is to love their children. In these commandments, God addressed the Israelites in a spirit of love. We can never lose sight of that fact. The Israelites, however, were not always a particularly loving people. At times they were so unloving as to turn from God to the worship of idols. Nevertheless, God reached out to them in love. He recognized them for what and who they are, but still loved them unconditionally. Parents who represent God's authority will love their children for *who they are*, rather than for *what they might do*. In fact, we might hate some of the *things* our children do, while loving the child who does them.

We remember, moreover, that God's commandments set out the conditions for maintaining loving relationships with God and with others. Honorable parents will also give their children rules and guidelines based in love. But they will love their children whether these rules are met or not. When children fail to follow godly rules, or even when they deliberately reject them, the parents may feel a great deal of sorrow. They will probably also feel a sense of failure. But their honorable parenting is not dependent upon what the children do with it. And whatever their children do, no matter how desperately the parents disagree with or fight against it, they will still love their children.

2. To Direct

Separate loving, for the moment, from what we might call "directing," or what the book of Proverbs describes as training a child in the way he or she should go. The love prevails, even when the directing seems to fail. And, regardless of whether the directing succeeds or not, it remains the responsibility of parents to direct their children. In fact, the task of supplying directions is a sign of their love.

A lack of directing, or letting a child do anything he or she pleases, may be a sign of lack of love or, at best, a sadly misdirected love. In Isaiah 38:19, the prophet says, "The living, the living—they praise you, as I am doing today; fathers tell their children of your faithfulness." So too, Christian parents have the responsibility to instruct their children in the fear and faithfulness of the Lord, recognizing that love is not a passive emotion but an active commitment to seek the right thing for the child.

We can see that also in Proverbs 6:20, which reads, "My son, keep your father's commands, and do not forsake your mother's teaching." And verse 23 says, "For these commands are a lamp, and this teaching is a light, and the reproofs of discipline are the way of life." So a Christian parent, one who honors the authority of God and acts honorably to the child, will actively and lovingly direct the child. Moreover, directing implies that parents also provide reproof or discipline for errancy.

Directing takes on several layers of meaning then. At its most immediate level, it is steering our children toward and in the right path. We want them to have a loving relationship with God, so we direct them toward it. At a second level, we recognize that our children will have a tendency to stray from that path, some for great distances. In such cases, through our love and our prayers for them and our actions toward them, we need to direct them home. Finally, at a third level, our parental directing consists of the models we provide for our children. In this sense, we are almost like directors of a choir, demonstrating in voice and action a relationship with God.

3. To Nurture

Honorable parents will also nurture their children. Nurturing involves something other than discipline or direction. To direct means, as the verse from Proverbs suggests, giving specific guidelines for right living. Discipline includes the actions taken when the directions are violated. Nurturing, however, focuses on the special gifts and needs of each individual child. Nurturing involves a special, individual attention that helps the child believe he or she is a special creation, uniquely gifted by God and especially worthy. While direction offers general guidelines for right and wrong that apply to all children, nurturing is guidance and support for the *individual* child according to his or her own special needs and gifts.

The fact of the matter is that each child is different, and along with that recognition comes the awareness that nurture will take different forms and differing amounts of time, depending on the child. Parents and children will need to see that equal love underlies all forms of nurture. Some children may have special needs that require more nurturing than another child, but each receives the same love.

We thus see three responsibilities of the honorable parent: to love, to direct, and to nurture their children. Now, how does the child honor the honorable parent? The answer grows directly from the parents' responsibilities: by obeying their direction, and by nurturing and loving those parents in return.

The Tasks of Children Who Honor

For many people this commandment to honor parents is reduced to a simple order: *obey* them. While obedience is certainly part of honoring, it is only a part, not the whole.

1. To Obey Direction

Obedience nurtures the loving relationship behind this commandment. It recognizes authority in the home as coming from God, through parents, to children. It is the essential glue that holds the family together. Obedience receives and follows loving parental direction—that responsibility of honorable parents. Disobedience not only untracks family harmony, it diminishes the authority of parents and, ultimately, of God.

Obedience may, at times, include doing hard things. Here we have a clear model in Jesus. In the garden at Gethsemane Jesus prayed in agony over the cross that awaited him. We read in Luke 22:42 that he prayed, "Father, if you are willing, take this cup from me; yet not my will, but yours be done." Here is the most remarkable act of obedience in all history. In honoring their parents, children may also have to obey hard directions and to make sacrifices of personal interests in order to obey. But when those directions have been given in love, obedience will result in blessings for the children and harmony in the home.

2. To Nurture

When children obey their parents they are also nurturing their parents in the responsibilities that God entrusted them with. But nurturing is more than simple obedience. Nurturing involves the recognition of individual, special gifts, and is also, therefore, practical. Children can nurture their parents in very practical ways, by complimenting them, for example, on special achievements; by expressing appreciation for what they have done; by saying "thanks" for the gifts and favors they give; and by telling them, over and over, how much they are loved.

A simple example, found in countless households, can make this clear. When there are young children scurrying around a house, there also seems to be artwork taped to walls, doors, and refrigerators. We lavish praise on each new creation, however uncertain we may be about what it is. Once, when she was only three, my daughter, Tamara, gave me a picture that caught my eye because part of it seemed to be trying awfully hard to look like letters. "Are these words, Tammy?" I asked her. Yes, they were. "Why don't you read them for me?" I asked. With great pride she read, "I love my dad." I still have that picture in my drawer, even though Tammy is a grown woman now. I still treasure the words.

Something happens to us as we grow up and leave one home to form a new one. Then, as we face questions and decisions about our own children, we begin, perhaps, to remember—this is how Mom did it. Or, Dad helped me get through this. And we realize that it is time to tell our parents "thanks" all over again, to nurture them by appreciating who they are and what they've done for us.

3. To Love

This nurturing of honorable parents is a matter of showing appreciation, but it is also part of a larger spirit. We honor our parents by loving them. That seems so obvious that perhaps it should be first on our list of ways to honor parents. But reversing the order may help us understand *how* to love parents, or what constitutes honorable love. While love always remains a divine goal for humans, it is also often clouded by human realities. Exercising or practicing love is different from mere wishfulness. Sometimes honorable love gets confused with slave-like obedience; sometimes it gets confused by decidedly dishonorable circumstances. Two items bear consideration here: the need for forgiveness when love goes awry, and the responsibilities that children bear when love is simply absent.

Loving Forgiveness

Mary was twenty-three years old, returning to college after several years of work in an automobile factory. She was unmarried—and certain that she never would marry. She was attractive, blessed with a witty personality that often bordered on cockiness, and had a first-rate mind. But she would never marry, not this Mary.

The problem was that her father had been killed during the fall of Vietnam, just days before the country collapsed and all U.S. personnel were evacuated. The irony of losing a father in a losing cause days before the whole affair collapsed was not lost on Mary. A cruel thing, but even more cruel because Mary had to grow up without a father. She remembered just enough about him to be angry at him, bitterly, gutwrenchingly angry at him for leaving her without a daddy.

Oh, Mary knew all the reasons why this feeling was wrong. She was, as I said, a bright woman. She certainly knew that it wasn't his fault. She also knew, with certainty, her mother's love for both her and her dead father. But the absence—that long, terrible void—had grown like a chasm between all that she knew and what she felt.

Psychologists have a relatively simple way of explaining this phenomenon. Being unable to express her anger at the situation that created it, Mary had to transfer that anger to a person—her dead father. Psychologists have a less easy task of leading someone like Mary to an understanding of that transfer, to a release of anger, and to a forgiveness of her father, herself, and, yes, God.

Forgiveness is a way of letting go, but it may be the single hardest action of a Christian life, simply because it is our human tendency to cling to and nurture harms done to us. They seethe in our memory like a cauldron. Even when we believe we have the lid locked down tight, some distant memory can bubble out, igniting once again the fires of anger and bitterness. The very heat of those fires, however, underscores the need to forgive.

Forgiveness is the first action to personal health, and ultimately to the ability to love. Forgiving is letting go of the emotions that block our own well-being. Forgiveness is an act of spiritual surgery in which we cleanse our nature of the pent-up wrongs that we cling to. There are two important points I want to make here regarding forgiveness in one's family life.

First, some people say they have to forgive "just for their own peace of mind." Let's be very clear about this. There are times when forgiveness *itself* causes anguish; it is seldom easy. If forgiveness is offered only for one's own peace of mind, it is highly doubtful that it is forgiveness. And it is highly doubtful that such "forgiveness" will lead to peace of mind. Our model here, as in all things in our Christian life, is Jesus. In every New Testament account of his forgiveness, it was always for the sake of others. His own "peace of mind" never entered into the picture.

Second, while we are often told "to forgive and forget," I doubt that this advice is wise, either spiritually or psychologically. Through the powerful love that Jesus gives us, we can forgive others for wrongs they have done to us. Forgetting about those wrongs, however, can be more difficult. And, provided that we don't harbor bitterness or a sense of self-pride, the memories of the forgiven wrong can make the power of Jesus' love seem even richer to us.

While the ideal remains for children to show honor by returning love to honorable parents, Mary's example demonstrates the human reality of a love often thwarted, sometimes twisted, by the frailties of our human condition. A theology that fails to account for that condition will always be insufficient. The comfort of the Ten Commandments, we realize once again, lies in their revelation of God's enduring love for us despite the frailties of our human condition. *We* need forgiveness.

That conflict between the divine ideal and human reality also bears relevance for parents and children at a time when so many homes are dysfunctional. For example, what about a child whose parents offer precious little direction or nurturing? Suppose a child is left pretty much to grow up on his or her own? There was such a child in my neighborhood when I was growing up, a fact that the rest of us children envied with an almost palpable jealously. He was our beacon of freedom because he had no rules. He never had a set time to be in, for example. Sometimes he would just walk around to see how late he could stay out before someone noticed.

But there was a darker side to his shining freedom. He couldn't ever remember his folks doing anything with him, unless they had to take him along on a trip because they couldn't find a place to leave him. When his parents came home at night, Dad would plunk down at the TV and Mom would pop a few TV dinners in the oven and run off to some meeting. The boy we all envied grew up with a cloud of morose defiance about him. He was cared for in a desultory sort of way, but he never experienced a sense of genuine love.

If asked whether they loved their son, his parents surely would have said yes. But they simply did not demonstrate that love in any tangible way. Like Mary, this young man also felt a huge absence, even though his parents were very much alive. Like Mary, he will need to learn how to forgive.

Sharing honorable love isn't easy; it's something one works at. One well-known author has said that, as a minimum for establishing a loving relationship with their children, parents should practice three ways of showing love to their children each day. First, they must give focused attention to each child—by really listening, by talking at the child's level, and meeting them where they are. The second is called loving eye contact. The way we look at our children tells a big story—do they see angry eyes, hurt eyes, bitter eyes, busy eyes, or loving eyes? And the third is touch—to hug or hold or touch the child in a loving way. Those are physical evidences of love. They are fairly simple exercises. But even these minimal expressions do not exist in many homes, and the effect of their absence can be devastating.

Parents Who Abuse

How does this commandment about honoring parents speak to families in which a mother or father actively abuse their role and responsibility to their children? Do the children still honor parents who, instead of directing, mislead; instead of nurturing, harm; instead of loving, abuse? Does a child honor such parents by submitting obediently? Is that what the commandment tells us? It might, if taken out of context from the other commandments and viewed apart from the God who gave it. But by arguing this way, one misses the context of the commandments as a whole: these are guides to happiness issued by a God who loves us dearly. When parents dishonor God, their children may very well have no other recourse than *not* to obey them. Ephesians 6:1 says, "Children, obey your parents in the Lord, for this is right." *In the Lord* is the important phrase. In the same vein, we are told in Mark 3:35 that "Whoever does God's will is my brother and sister and mother," which suggests that the family of Christ is a believer's primary family.

In one of the most troubling sayings of Jesus, recorded in Matthew 10:35-37, we are told, "For I have come to set a man against his father, and a daughter against her mother, and a daughter-in-law against her mother-in-law—a man's enemies will be the members of his own household. He who loves father or mother more than me is not worthy of me; and he who loves son or daughter more than me is not worthy of me." Such passages seem to speak directly to the question. If parents dishonor Christ, the child's duty and honor are forfeit them. Always, always our honor is *first* directed to God. This is not a pattern to be taken frivolously, but it does bear important implications. If parents require the child to do something in clear violation of God's commandments, the child's first responsibility is to God.

Perhaps you can see where this is leading. Many homes have children honoring honorable parents; many homes do not. That is precisely what makes the *family of God*—the church—so important. Truly enacted, the church is a home for the homeless, a family for those who do not have a family, or who do not have a family that honors God. Here is a place where we can all practice this commandment: within God's church we are all parents, sisters, sons, daughters, to one another. This is our way of caring for those who are homeless. And it includes—but goes beyond—such facilities as food pantries for needy families, shelter for those who need it, a sanctuary for abused mothers and children.

And this brings us back, finally, to those people who make their way to Heartside Clinic. They are standing in line already early in the morning. Sometimes they are holding homemade bandages over wounds received the night before. In winter, they huddle together while the wind whips snow down Division Avenue. They are together in their common loss. They are homeless.

Not infrequently I am walking with my wife when one of the street people from Heartside greets her warmly. One of these is Richard. Richard is always alone. He is short and stocky; his face, where the whiskers don't hide it, is laced with scars. Richard has had a rough life. His roughest enemy has been alcohol. Although he has stayed at a long string of missions, his closest family member appears to be a jug of wine.

About a mile and a half from the Heartside Clinic, still within the confines of what we call the "inner city," is Madison Square Church. Madison Square is not a church for everyone, precisely because it is a church for anyone. Situated on the mean streets, it believes in bringing a ministry of Christ's love to those streets.

We were surprised one Sunday when Richard walked into Madison Square Church. His sweater was tattered, his pants baggy and dirty. He had come for the early service. He stayed for Sunday school, which my wife and I were leading that day. He hugged Pat after the session. He entered a seven-day prayer compact with me for his alcoholism. He stayed for the second service. After it was over, Richard went forward to give his life to Jesus.

He has been back regularly. I don't know if his struggles with alcohol are over. He is still homeless—but not entirely. He has found a home he can always return to, and a family who gives him love and lovingly receives him as he is. That's a place to call home. More, he has found a father, and a brother: he has found Jesus. Richard is in a safe place now—a home for the spirit that will be there for all eternity. He is part of a family.

REFLECTIONS

1. This commandment shifts focus in God's Law, moving from our relationship with God to our relationships with others. Why does this "second table of the law" begin with a commandment for families?

   How do you define "family"?

   Who are the members of your family?

2. The opening pages about the people at Heartside Clinic are a poignant account of people without homes. How does this commandment apply to their lives?

   Under this commandment, do we have a special responsibility to them?

   In what way are many of us also "homeless"—struggling to find a sense of home and family in our lives?

3. In recent years much has been written about the disintegration of the family structure. Even more has been written about "dysfunctional families." Think carefully about the families you know—your own and those of people around you. How do you feel about the family structure in your world?

   What do you see as the root of family problems today?

4. The chapter talks about "honorable parents" and "children who honor." Although the commandment seems to be addressed to children, what heavy responsibilities does it lay upon parents?

Think about your own parents—your biological parents or anyone else who has "parented" you as God's representatives. What are some ways in which they have guided and directed you into a closer relationship with God?

5. Three key responsibilities for "honorable parents" are to *love, direct,* and *nurture* their children. How are directing and nurturing inseparable from loving?

Again think about your own relationship with your parents. How did you nurture your parents when you were a child? How can you nurture them now?

6. Although it is not mentioned specifically in the commandment, forgiveness is an essential part of any family relationship, of any "honoring" among family members. Many self-help books have been written to help children from dysfunctional families understand and cope with abusive family relationships. How is an understanding of Christian forgiveness essential in any such "help"?

What are some specific ways that the Church—the body of Christ—can carry out this commandment in its relationship with people who are without home or loving families?

6

Bearing the Image of God

You shall not murder.

EXODUS 20:13

With our myriad of different personalities, each of us tends to see things just a bit differently and to hold to what we see with differing strengths. One person might be adamantly certain he has the right view; another never stops questioning his view.

I've often thought how nice it would be never to have a question about religious matters. Or, better yet, to have all the answers. Some people believe they do. Others may have questions but don't dare admit to them. Some people believe they have questions that they will want to ask God when they get to heaven, forgetting that when they get to heaven our earthly questions will be meaningless.

Yet it is important to our Christian life to be able to raise our questions honestly and to search for answers. We do not have to be afraid of that. Sometimes people lock positions into black and white because they are afraid of exploring the gray areas of their minds. This understanding is important because the four simple words of this commandment evoke so many, and such strongly held views. Perhaps because those contrasting views are held so strongly, we become fearful of speaking to the issues at all.

I'm afraid of two kinds of people: those who have all the answers and those who have stopped asking questions. With God, we enter a safe place where we can raise our questions and search his answers. As long as we confess the absolute authority of God, and are guided by Scripture, we can—we *must*—explore those gray areas of uncertainty that seem to appear to most of us.

So very many ambiguities seem to surround the commandment against murder. Yet one senses here a profound simplicity: Do not murder. Just that.

The Hard Issues

Working one's way through the gray areas surrounding our application of this commandment would require a text many pages longer than this one. The issues pile up in number and complexity. Consider just a few of these issues.

One such area involves dietary matters, and this is not a light issue for many Christians who have chosen to become vegetarians in protest against the frequently painful means of producing meat to suit consumer tastes. For them, the slaughter of livestock is a kind of "murder," and they take their stand against it by consuming a vegetarian diet.

A second area of ambiguity, the issue of "just" war, has become far more controversial. Here the issue involves the slaughter of human lives. The staggering toll of suffering and death from wars in our century almost numbs our senses. We don't want *another* war, not after the horrors of Vietnam, not after the brutality of Korea, not after the flames of world wars. But then we think also of dictators and warlords executing people by the thousands, and we wonder what we are to do.

In yet a third way, modern society divides itself into gray areas when it addresses capital punishment. Who decides when one individual merits capital punishment? Is there a difference between a murderer who takes the life of one person or the one who takes the life of twenty-seven when it comes to meting punishment?

And still another area of controversy in today's society is the act of euthanasia. Some world governments permit the prescription of drugs by which an individual can end his or her life. Many states in our own nation are now debating the legal and moral issues of permitting "passive" euthanasia, providing the means but not the direct intervention for a person to end his or her own life. Obvious legal issues, as well as moral issues, apply, for the U.S. Constitution asserts the right to life, liberty, and happiness for each citizen. Is it possible that when an individual's happiness is abrogated by suffering, then the right to life is waived also? But who determines the degree of suffering? Is it a chronic, debilitating illness, or a mere inability to sustain a certain lifestyle to which one has become accustomed?

And, finally, one of the deepest ethical and spiritual issues related to this commandment, one which has cut through our nation and through people's hearts like a scythe, is the practice of abortion. The questions twist and turn with cyclonic force, and people—even people in the church—are blown apart into polarized camps.

Maybe, instead of arguing the pros and cons of any of these issues at length, it will be more helpful to approach all issues of life in another way. As from the outset of our study, we want to remember the positive force of the commandment, that which brings us into a closer walk with our living and loving God.

The Positive Force of the Commandment

Since the thematic unity of the Ten Commandments lies not in a mere list of proscribed behavior, but in God's revelation of his loving-kindness and his directions for maintaining a loving relationship with him, this commandment against murder should first be seen in its positive application. That positive application is guided considerably by the later commandment of Jesus to love our enemies, and to love even those who despitefully use us and persecute us. That's pretty hard to do, virtually impossible apart from God's grace, yet Jesus did it on the cross when he prayed for those who were putting him to death: "Father, forgive them."

There is, however, another framework that provides guidance for this one particular commandment. God is the author of life, and as Creator he is supreme authority. We asked earlier in whose likeness humanity is made, and answered, "in the likeness of God" who is the life-giver. Having been made in God's likeness, then, humanity is supposed to be a life-giver, not a life-taker.

We note again that this law falls under the second table: human responsibilities toward other humans—individuals made in the image of God in relation to other image-bearers of God. God tells us that our responsibility is to love one another in the pattern set by the one in whose image we all are made. We lay down our lives for our neighbors rather than take their lives.

Jesus' parable of the good Samaritan specifically informs us that we are to love our neighbor, and Jesus adds that hatred for our neighbor is as bad as actual murder. In his sermon on the mountain, Jesus reminded the listeners: "But I tell you that every one who is angry with his brother shall be subject to judgment. . . . But anyone who says, 'You fool!' shall be liable to the hell of fire" (Matthew 5:22).

Murder, the taking of innocent life, is clearly a violation of this commandment, but Jesus makes it clear that the *denigration of any person* is subject to divine judgment under this commandment. The bitterness of hatred, the cruelty of mockery—these damage the image of God in the person against whom they are directed. When we ignore the pain of the downtrodden, when we are insensitive to need, when we turn our back upon hurt—we damage the image of God in another person. Mean-spiritedness, cynicism, the cutting remark—these, too, are forms of murder. We may never excuse ourselves by saying, "I haven't slain anyone; therefore I am okay by this commandment." The Bible doesn't permit that. God's love doesn't permit it.

Here is the heart of the matter, then: our responsibility under the commandment is to not murder anyone, and our responsibility under Jesus' interpretation of the commandment is to love everyone. The commandment may be seen as having two sides, to avoid harm and to enact love.

Because our human nature tries to turn us against the life God wants and offers, we need the negative proscriptions ("thou shalt not") to help us see what we *should* do—for peace, for happiness, for closeness with God.

Just as each of us has been guilty of breaking this commandment through thoughtless or intentional words and actions that destroy and cripple life, so also we have all been victims of sins against the commandment. I learned a profound lesson about a kind of dying—a loss of life—when I was a young boy. The thoughts that arose as I explored this commandment echoed memories of that day when I died.

It is not the dying of the body I am speaking of. It is a death with its own fierce pain—the death of the spirit. It happened like this:

I grew up during the 1950s in one of those quintessential American communities that really had no identity because it changed so rapidly. It was, for the most part, a good neighborhood to grow up in. There were enough kids around to get up a game of baseball nearly any summer afternoon on the playground of the local school. Neat, unpretentious homes stood side by side along the tree-lined streets. A good neighborhood, and one changing almost daily with the influx of immigrants attracted to its affordable housing. I can remember trailing along behind my mother innumerable times as she delivered fresh-baked rolls to a newly arrived family. I was as hungry for friends as the newcomers were for rolls.

By the time I was in third grade I was a typical kid—gangly, uncoordinated, sporting my first pair of glasses in frames as thick as rubber tires, desperately insecure, frantically curious about the world, grateful to anyone who would call me a friend and share some time with me.

At about that time, a family moved in six blocks away from us. It was a slovenly, narrow house they lived in, this family I'll call the Beukemas. It stood across from a cemetery, on a dirt yard pock-marked by the diggings of one of the neighborhood strays.

The Beukemas had a son, Theo. And he was my age. I was grateful for this potential new friend. I guided him at school, sitting near his desk to help him with language problems. I invited him over to my house to play after school. He was willing—eager—to come, but he was as secretive as a shadow.

3. Take the commandment into your own experience and life. Jesus tells us that the denigration of any person is subject to divine judgment under this commandment. The bitterness of hatred, the cruelty of mockery—these damage the image of God in the person against whom they are directed. How are such actions also "murders"—how do they kill another person?

4. Recall the story of the author's childhood experience with Theo Beukema. On the basis of the above understanding, who was the victim and who was the culprit in that story? Who took a life, and who suffered a kind of death?

   How did the author's adult understanding change his feelings about that incident?

   Think back to similar experiences of "death" that you have had. Think carefully about how they affected you and others. What do you discover about the meaning and the intent of the commandment against murder?

5. Now turn the commandment around. If its negative, or *proscriptive*, command is against murder, what is it telling us we *should* do? Compose a simple sentence that expresses the positive, *prescriptive*, side of the commandment.

6. How can this positive understanding of the commandment guide your feelings and interactions with others? How might it guide your feelings about those explosive issues mentioned in question 2?

Even then I sensed something was wrong. Too often when he left, I felt a coldness rather than warmth. But I didn't understand those feelings, not in third grade. I was puzzled and confused when I noticed several toys of mine missing after one of his visits. I didn't know what to do about it. I didn't want to do anything that would risk our friendship.

Finally, one day he invited me to his house after school. Because Theo rode his bicycle the half mile to school, we stopped by my house to pick up my bike. It was double excitement—riding a bike to a friend's house.

I remember how cold it seemed when we entered his house. There was no one else home. No parent calling hello. No after-school snack. Theo was chattering nervously. We climbed narrow stairs to his bedroom. It was bare and gloomy up there. His room was a small cube at the end of the hall, a broken shade hung from the one dirty window.

He opened the door, letting me go in first. The room stood in shadows.

He had made no effort to hide them. He stood waiting, his eyes fierce, until I saw them. His bed was a mattress on the floor. His dresser was a wooden box. And on the box were my missing toys. I heard the door shut behind me.

I don't remember all the words now. I remember choking, "Those are mine."

"You wanna bet?" he said. His fists were clenched.

He stood in front of the closed door, slowly pulling the leather belt from his waist. He wrapped it around one hand, the buckle dangling.

"I think I better go," I said.

He shook his head. Then, the words that burned like acid in my ears. "I hate you," he hissed.

As he dangled the belt, he said, "I'm going to kill you." I stared, unbelieving, into his eyes. Two dark coals burning.

He lifted the belt. Then stopped. "Wanna see what it feels like?" he snarled. Suddenly he dropped his baggy pants and turned around. His buttocks, his upper thighs, were a welter of stripes, deep purple and red bruises, some old, some still raw-edged and scabbed.

I sucked in a terrible breath and bolted. While he stood there, pants down, I ripped open the door and ran. As I careened down the steps he screamed after me, "Hey, come back! I didn't . . ."

Then I was pounding the bike back toward Neland Avenue.

At school we avoided each other, pretending nothing had happened, pretending we didn't even know each other, pretending the other was not there. So it went for a long year. The next year he didn't return to my school.

But for a long time those words burned in my mind: "I hate you."

His words were knives in my heart. Something died in my spirit that day.

Not for many years did I begin to understand. Perhaps it finally came to me one night when I lay awake thinking of my own children. Suddenly that old memory came crawling out of the past. And suddenly I began to understand. Someone else—someone he wanted to call *friend*—had spoken those enraged words to him as a belt fell and lacerated his flesh. As someone stole a part of his life away. We had both been victims of those who broke the commandment about taking life.

Then I regretted that I had not been brave enough to stay.

I was only a boy at that time. But even now I don't know if I am all that much braver before such words that destroy and slay the spirit. I would still want to run away, run home.

REFLECTIONS

The commandment against murder may, at first readin to be the most straightforward law and the easiest to But when we apply its spirit and intent to our lives, v step into many "gray areas" of uncertainty.

1. At the beginning of this chapter, the author says, "Sometimes people lock positions into black and v because they are afraid of exploring the gray area; their minds." Do you think it's also true that it's ea see things in "black and white" when those things outside our immediate experience—when they inv issues we have never personally experienced?

2. It is important in any consideration of the explosiv issues touched by this commandment—euthanasia, capital punishment, and abortion, in particular—th are guided by a clear awareness of two things in e measure: *the sanctity of life in God's sight, and the of love that underlies all these commandments*.

With those two things in mind, consider your feelin; about the issues of euthanasia, capital punishment, abortion. How do you feel about each issue? Why d feel the way you do? Look very carefully at the moti that underlie your feelings. How is a respect for san life balanced with a spirit of God's love in your feeli

What is the best way to express your feelings abou those issues? Make a list of tactics that you feel are appropriate and effective. How do you approach s one who does not share your views?

How does the important Christian concept of forgiv enter into any feelings or actions related to these is:

7

Keeping Promises

You shall not commit adultery.

EXODUS 20:14

Small Town Voices

I remember him for his faithfulness. But that is only part of him. Mr. Leroy Uber was one of three really wise men I have known in my life, although I didn't know that when I first met him. That is the way with wisdom; it appears always unexpectedly, a gift, often in strange and unusual human packages. This package was undersize, a rather small and compact man, save for the very large shoulders. His shirts were worn smooth about the shoulders from the firm muscles working against the material. He wore an old green shirt of shiny, cottony material, and brown gabardine pants, always clean. He had a large head, thin, white hair combed neatly to one side, wide eyes, a kind of pulpy nose, and thick lips that broke easily into a grin even when he held a pipe between clenched teeth. He used an old Prince Albert can for his tobacco, its red coating worn nearly through to flat, gray metal. I once bought him a two-pound can of Prince Albert, which he accepted graciously. Some time later I learned that he smoked Edgeworth, but simply liked that handy little tin can to carry it in. What I thought of then simply as graciousness, I now recognize as part of his faithfulness. Mr. Uber kept true to honoring others.

Long, almost apelike arms hung along his short body. His hands were thick and puffy, with broad, spatulate fingers. The tendon on his right thumb stretched even from the first joint to the base of his index finger. The thumb was bent crookedly inward. These things you noticed immediately, and when you shook the gnarled hand you felt the tough ridge of tendon in your palm.

After knowing him for some months, he explained about that tendon when he helped me edge my new concrete driveway. He was there to help—a faithful man. The driveway then was simply a muddy gravel path. He believed we could do it in concrete. Do it together.

Mud from the holes in the old driveway was always tracked into the house; the children needed a clean, hard place to play. We would have a concrete driveway. Three friends and I were pegging down the forms when Mr. Uber came over. He watched while we nailed the wire mesh to the gravel bed, nodding approvingly.

"Hello," I said, leaning on a two-by-four.

"Hello. Ever done this before?"

"No, but we're going to try."

"You're doing fine. Got tools?"

"Tools?"

"Bull float? Edging blades? You're welcome to use my tools. If you like, I'll edge it for you. Told you we could do it together."

I had forgotten his offer.

It was the way he offered it now that struck me; not like the old pro showing off for the obviously ignorant. He wanted to help, but he was wise enough to let it be my choice and my design. He came back from his narrow, green house across the street with a load of tools under each arm.

"Help yourself," he said, but he kept the finish-edger in his hand. These were not the makeshift tools to which I had become accustomed; they were the tools of a professional— worn, weathered, the hickory handles smooth from long use, and each spotlessly clean.

We finished the forms and waited for the concrete truck; leaning on rakes, hoes, and shovels, the morning air holding a crisp, cold bite of autumn. Mr. Uber had changed to old jeans and high rubber boots. He had rubber gloves stained a flat gray from years of concrete lime. Someone poured coffee from a thermos, and its rich scent rose like perfume in the quiet air.

"How does it look to you, Mr. Uber?"

"Good. Good. You boys do it good."

"You've done this before?"

"I guess so," he admitted. "For about sixty-five years, more or less. I was a brickmason. That's how I got this." He held out his crooked hand. "See, I worked on chimneys at the steel mills. When you had to corner brick, you'd hold it in that hand and rap it with the hammer. Hit it right and you had a perfect cut. That tendon there was the ridge I broke on. Gave a perfect cut. Broke the hand out of shape in time, though. Sixty-five years." He looked wistfully at the sky. "You're going to have a good clear day."

Then the truck lumbered up, the sluice extended, and the thick, gray wave of concrete spewed out. Shoulders began to ache with shoveling. Push and heave. Work that hoe.

Mr. Uber watched, nodding and smiling. He took the big float and touched some rough spots. They disappeared like magic. He stood and tapped the edger against his knee. "We'll do her now," he said suddenly through a cloud of tobacco smoke, and with deft, urgent strokes separated the gray concrete, gave it definition and shape. He moved steadily, quickly, precisely. We drank coffee and nodded appreciatively.

He rose and handed me the edger. "You get to top off the last edge," he said. I knelt at his feet and, with clumsy imitations, sawed at the concrete. He nodded. "You're getting it. Fine. Just fine."

Although I didn't recognize it at the time, he had given me the first, simple lesson of wisdom. He showed me a way to go, then let me go it in my own stumbling way. His voice was at the back of my mind, pointing. A lesson in faithfulness also. There is more to the lesson of Mr. Uber. But already I see implications for this commandment. Above all, the commandment is about growing in the wisdom of God by keeping faithfulness to one's marriage partner. Mr. Uber taught me much about such fidelity. To understand the meaning of faithfulness, one first has to understand the great good blessing that is marriage and, second, the full implications of adultery.

The Meaning of Adultery

Sometimes we want to skip right over this commandment, and go directly to the one on stealing. Nearly all of us have stolen something in our lifetime, so that commandment's application seems more direct and immediate. Until, that is, we begin to define and understand adultery—a term everyone thinks he or she understands but few bother to define.

A dictionary definition would offer something like, "Violation of a marriage by one of the partners having sexual intercourse with someone outside the marriage." That's off the top of my head, but it demonstrates the problem with all definitions—trying to squeeze a universe of meaning into few words. It's a starting point, but there's more involved.

This commandment involves keeping faith, or allegiance, an action that is foundational to the whole of the Ten Commandments but especially pertinent to this one. Certainly being faithful is crucial to marriage, since sexual relations are an important part of a sound marriage. But marriage is more than sexual relations. What is the basis for a Christian marriage? Rather than beginning by looking at the negative act of adultery, it may be helpful first to examine the positive institution of which adultery is a violation—marriage.

The Biblical Pattern for Marriage

My wife and I have had the blessing of celebrating, with each set of our parents, their fiftieth wedding anniversaries. In some ways, we found it more giddy, more joyful and exhilarating than a marriage itself. A marriage celebrates the embarkation upon what is expected to be a long voyage of faithfulness. An anniversary, especially one like the fiftieth, celebrates the course of that voyage, the blessing of faithfulness enacted.

Most amusing, however, were tales of early dating, courtship, and marriage that these two sets of lovers shared during the celebrations. Inevitably, it turned each listener back upon his or her own experience.

At least, it surely did to me.

I remembered a bitterly cold January night many years before, way back in high school, when a wholly unexpected thing happened. The younger sister of one of my best friends, a girl I would phone once in a while to get leads on dates with other girls, called *me* and asked me out. I was surprised, but I agreed. It might be fun.

We "doubled" with another couple. Pat took me tobogganing. Outside. In that bitter cold. Down long icy shoots, then a half-mile hike back up the hill. And we rode crammed in the backseat of a VW Beetle with a heater as powerful as a fly's gasping.

It was the best night of my life.

I've told Pat I fell in love with her right there. Right then.

Well, she didn't fall in love with me right there and right then. In fact, for her it was a process that deepened steadily until five years later when we married.

Did our marriage start on that first night? Or whenever it was we fell in love? Or when I proposed? Or when she agreed? No. *It started when we pledged our faithfulness to each other in the vows we took before God.*

I emphasize that sentence, underscore it. Marriage is not about emotions, not about meeting needs or compatibility, not about sexuality. Marriage is about keeping faithfulness— to each other and to God. And the reasons for this high premium on faithfulness go back to a very early time.

This fundamental structure for God's divine order begins in the very act of creation. In Genesis 2 we read that God created Eve to make a "helper *suitable* for Adam." Nothing in the animal world was suitable; nothing else bore God's image. This fact Adam recognizes when he says, "This at last is bone of my bones and flesh of my flesh." A union. A perfect match. It was a glorious suitability, this gift God bestowed upon Adam and Eve and all humanity, a gift from a loving God.

To mark the glory of this union, a special event of festivity and ceremony is called for. Thus, marriage is established in Genesis 2:24, "Therefore a man leaves his father and his mother and cleaves to his wife, and they become one flesh." The formal ceremony of marriage is supported by Jesus in Matthew 19:4-6: "'Haven't you read that at the beginning the Creator made them male and female,' and said, 'For this reason a man will leave his father and mother and be joined to his wife, and the two will become one flesh'? So they are no longer two but one flesh. What therefore God has joined together, let no man put asunder."

I remember again Mr. Uber and the concrete driveway on that morning long ago. Just as we set the forms for the concrete, God sets parameters for human marriage. These give new life; they provide shape and definition. And, as Mr. Uber formed the edges that shaped the concrete, so this commandment edges the specialness of a new life together, within but apart from the world. The act of marriage is not only supported but also celebrated in other passages of Scripture. One thinks especially of how Jesus joined in the celebration of marriage at a wedding feast in the town of Cana. He performed one of his first miracles there, simply to add to the joy of the occasion.

Marriage as Faithfulness

Something larger than simply physical or emotional attraction is involved in marriage, then. Keeping faithfulness in marriage parallels keeping faithfulness to God. A rupture in the marriage vow ultimately is a rupture of spiritual fidelity. Thus the sacredness of the marriage vow that is taken before God.

When we see the high regard for marriage in the Bible, we begin to understand the clear warnings against a violation of Christian marriage. This commandment is one evidence, but it is strongly supported elsewhere in Scripture. Deuteronomy 22:22 considers adultery so evil that the death

117

penalty is recommended: "If a man is found sleeping with another man's wife, both the man who slept with her and the woman must die. You must purge the evil from Israel." That's the same penalty for idolatry, by the way. The New Testament echoes a general warning in Hebrews 13:4: "Marriage should be honored by all, and the marriage bed kept pure, for God will judge the adulterer and all the sexually immoral."

Idolatry and Adultery

The action of idolatry is ever the same. Humans follow their own needs and desires rather than God's will. The reason for adultery is similar. A marriage partner follows his or her own needs and desires rather than the sanctity of the marriage vow made before God. It occurs in so many insidious ways: from a growing apart by letting marriage degenerate from a mystery of grace to mere manners of custom, to the abrupt wrenching action of an adulterous relationship. In each case, the spiritual action is the same: a turning from faithfulness to satisfy human desire.

Now, in the minds of some Christians, sexuality itself is a bad, nasty thing. It is something we can't help, a curse we have that has to be regulated by marriage. Instead of sex for the marriage's sake, we have marriage for the sake of sex.

That negative attitude, however, runs counter to the testimony of Scripture. The Bible regards human sexuality as a gift from God; and, like all his gifts, it is one that we can use in joy and freedom—within the marriage vow as biblically ordained. With total respect for each other, and lovingly submitting to each other, Christian marriage partners have a fully liberated sexuality.

If sex is a divine gift, and if it is a fundamental part of our human nature, then one might ask why we can't use it whenever we want—including outside of marriage. There are good reasons why many Christians believe that sexual relations should be limited to marriage. First, it is the natural order ordained by God himself. But we also need to understand what sexuality outside the bonds of marriage can lead to.

The Sex Urge

One reason why people may have sexual relationships outside of marriage is sheer loneliness. People need other people. Often the only thing they have in common is the human instinct to have sex. We might call this "desperation sex," because it grants a few hours or moments of close contact with another human. But it is only a kind of totem set up in place of genuine love.

When we discussed idolatry, we said it was always a response to individual needs and desires, but it never satisfies because those needs are boundless, always requiring more. Sex, when the boundaries and standards of marriage are forsaken, becomes an end in itself; however, it is one incapable of granting any sense of final satisfaction. Like idolatry it can become all-consuming, always insisting upon more, only granting momentary appeasement. In marriage *love* is the goal, not satisfaction.

The Bible doesn't talk about personal pleasure and "self-realization." It talks about faithfulness and the blessings that accrue from that faithfulness. A passage from the Old Testament book of Jeremiah bears special relevance to this issue. In fact, the passage strikes forcefully to the heart of all of the commandments. Jeremiah prophesied in Judah for four decades, during a time of political and moral degeneracy. He was a brave and deeply religious man who particularly spoke out against the false prophets who led his people astray. We have the false prophets of sexuality today who tell us that if it feels good, do it; who describe seventy-nine ways to feel good. Jeremiah counsels us about such false prophets.

This is what the Lord Almighty says: "Do not listen to what the prophets are prophesying to you; they fill you with false hopes.

They speak visions from their own minds, not from the mouth of the Lord. (Jeremiah 23:16-17)

There's more. Jeremiah continues a few verses later, after talking about the storm of God's anger about to break upon the liars:

"Am I only a God nearby," declares the Lord. "and not a God far away? Can anyone hide in secret places so that I cannot see him?" declares the Lord. "Do not I fill heaven and earth?" declares the Lord. "I have heard what the prophets say who prophesy lies in my name. They say, 'I had a dream! I had a dream!' How long will this continue in the hearts of these lying prophets, who prophesy the delusions of their own minds? They think the dreams they tell one another will make my people forget my name, just as their fathers forgot my name through Baal worship" (Jeremiah 23:23-27).

The passage ties any deceit, any deviation from God's will, to idolatry. But the larger pattern, the positive counterpart to adultery, lies in fidelity. And fidelity is a matter of the heart.

That's why Jesus says in Matthew 5:27-28: "You have heard that it was said, 'Do not commit adultery.' But I tell you that anyone who looks at a woman lustfully has already committed adultery with her in his heart." Adultery isn't simply an act of sex with someone other than the marriage partner. It is an action of the heart, a displacement of loyalty. It applies to singles as well as marriage partners.

Directions in the Modern Maze

Our age has made a kind of god of sex. It's a part of modern culture—the stuff of advertisements, the lifeblood of the industry, and it appears all around us. Television and films steam with scenes of illicit sex. When treated casually by the media, sexual promiscuity becomes a commonplace, routine, and often accepted part of life. It's hard to hold fidelity in an age that places no value upon it. That especially is why

Christians need tutoring and nurturing in the holy value of sex and marriage.

As with all Christian values, such tutoring and nurturing begin in the home. The family is, as we have mentioned, the cornerstone of God's kingdom on earth. Adultery is so dangerous because it's a crack in that cornerstone. How can children comprehend the fidelity of marital sex if their own parents abuse it?

But, someone might well object, all this talk about fidelity is making me nervous. Can't faithfulness of this sort be just another kind of slavery? Do I have to be faithful to my marriage partner in *everything*? Don't I have any rights?

Rights. Indeed you have rights. In fact, I believe a Christian marriage involves something of a Bill of Rights. If, as with the U.S. Bill of Rights, all rights are also *obligations*, then I set forth what I call a Marital Bill of Rights. But be clear here: anytime the word *right* is used, it can also be construed as *obligation*. This is an ethical covenant, a spiritual law. It is gender-inclusive, applying equally to either spouse, good for all times and places. It goes like this:

I have the right to say, "I'm sorry." You have the right to say, "You're forgiven."

I have the right to ask for a hug. You have the right to give me one.

I have the right to need some time to myself. You have the right to pick up my household obligations to give me time off.

I have the right to ask your permission to do something I really want to do. You have the right to grant it, knowing I really want to do it.

I have the right to treasure quiet moments, to love surprises, to be happy in the really peculiar things that make me happy. You have the right to understand my odd habits, my quirky customs, my joys, and to know they are a part of the person you love.

121

I have the right to weep. You have the right to just let me or to hold me. You'll know when. If you don't know when, I have the right to tell you.

I have the right to believe that nothing is more important than God. You have the right to let me act upon that belief as God leads me.

I have the right to say, "I love you." You have the right to tell me you love me.

I have the right to say, "Not now, please." You have the right to be there later.

I have the right to sacrifice for you. You have the right to lay down all your life, and whatever seems important to you, for me.

I have the right to care for you, to tend you when you are weak. You have the right to admit you need my care and that you are weak.

I have the right to grow flowers in our garden. You have the right to pick them.

And, I might add, *you* have the right to modify this list for practical applications of loving fidelity in whatever way suits the loyalties of your marriage. The point is that, in matters of marriage, we learn best from examples; then we apply these where appropriate to our individual lives. If we are always finding models, we must always find the ways they fit our marriages, for each marriage is unique. Manuals and books inform us and grant good examples, but it is the model standing before us in our own lives from which we learn best.

I am grateful to have had one such model early in my own marriage; it was, again, Mr. Uber. The day we laid concrete for the driveway wasn't the first time I had seen him. That only explains the crookedness of his thumb. Later that evening, while I watered the curing cement, he walked across from his house, and he took out a worn wallet. It held the obligatory pictures of a daughter and her family in California—"Like to go there sometime; doubt whether I will"—some old friends, and three or four pictures of him as a high tower man. He did chimneys in Pittsburgh, church steeples in Youngstown, cornices of the government buildings in Sharon. It made me dizzy to look up at him, waving a brick from the rim of a chimney—"one-hundred forty-seven feet, that one was."

But the first time I saw this muscular, elf-like man, I was the one balanced atop a forty-foot ladder, looking down at his tuft of white hair above the thick shoulders. That ladder, against whose higher rungs my feet trembled nervously, was propped against the first house I bought.

After seven years of marriage, two children, and virtually no savings, I had longed for a house in the way that Noah must have—not just a house; a place to rest, land to turn and plant, a view of trees from the window. The impediment, of course, was that there were virtually no savings. The realtor, a model of grace and financial understanding, had called one afternoon: "I think I have it." My interest picked up when he mentioned the price on the way to view the house: $17,500. This was 1973. Even a college teacher might swing that, I thought.

I remember seeing only a brown hulk broken by graceful swoops of roof line and an interesting array of grimy windows. I walked into the front foyer, noticed the mullioned windows through cobwebs and moss, and said, "I'll take it." Then, "Maybe we should show it to my wife," I added.

This house was like the Christmas present I had hoped for all my life, magnificently proportioned, full of ornate surprises, oddly shaped windows, curious built-in furnishings. It had been concocted by two Scottish sisters who immigrated during the Depression and wanted to model their New World home on their ancestral Scottish "cottage" but couldn't quite remember what it was like. My wife had stood incredulous in the living room and murmured softly, "Well, if you think you can do something about it . . ." What faith!

In six weeks, we had gutted it to the bone, installing a new bath, kitchen, carpeting, and so forth. The inside sparkled. We loved every hard-worked-for inch of that house. And so the house became a home.

The first time I saw my little neighbor was from the top of the ladder where I was staining warped shingles. From then on he was a part of that house, always unobtrusive, a little slow with suggestions, happy to offer or withhold. He had an eye for the lumber I used in remodeling. He would hold a piece of wood, peer down its grain, and say, "It's a good piece, but go gentle there. See how the grain works around the knot?"

"Yes," I said, shagging my eyebrow up and trying to look as he looked. "Yes."

"You know the wood by the grain. You can see where the hot summer, the hard winter worked on it. There's life in every wood. A history. You'll do all right if you work around that knot. All good wood has a knot in it."

All of life is like that; so, too, all marriages. Over the course of years knots appear in the grain. There are hard winters when the soul aches, dry summers when questions appear. Sometimes marriages suffer from an onslaught of temptations; sometimes a slow crookedness works at its flow. This commandment tells us to stick with the pattern—the knots just become little lumps in the grain, then, rather than a dissolution of the whole.

In time I finished the house-painting. Mr. Uber looked at my work, now shining with the forty-two gallons of primer and bright gold paint. "Sure looks good," he said. "Big daffodil."

I laughed. "Your own house could use some paint," I said. "I'll help you with it."

"All right. I'll pay you."

"We'll see about that."

The day I started painting Mr. Uber's house he fixed iced tea at 10 A.M. "Better cool down," he called from the foot of the ladder. "I've got iced tea made."

The kitchen was what I expected: old-fashioned red and white linoleum tiles, pale yellow walls, an aged ceramic sink and claw-footed stove. All immaculate. He handed me the ice-beaded glass. "Come in and make yourself comfortable," he said. "Meet my wife."

I hoped he didn't note my surprise; I didn't know he had a wife.

She was bundled in a living room chair, a tiny fluff of flesh packed in blankets. Her bright eyes twinkled like a nervous bird as she cocked her head. She seemed so frail, ready to fly away. "This is my wife," he said graciously, then added almost to himself, "though she can't hear, anyway."

Her eyes twinkled. Her head cocked. Her fragile hand, thin bones webbed by nearly translucent skin, waved feebly. At last a faint smile, as though worked up by an enormous effort of will, moved across her lips. Mr. Uber tucked the blankets around her.

He had cared for her, I learned later, in just such a way for many years. A quiet testimony to a quiet faithfulness.

The fierce winter that year died slowly. The late spring sun splashed mud puddles into silver streams that wound among snow mounds on Main Street. Our family walked the six blocks home from church on Sunday mornings.

In front of Mr. Uber's house one May morning, an ambulance rumbled, its red light flashing like a silent scream in the morning air.

I ran over as they lifted her tiny form into the ambulance, one hand feebly clawing the air. Mr. Uber stood in the doorway, rubbing his forehead disconnectedly with his gnarled hand.

"They're taking her to the hospital."

"Maybe she'll be all right."

"No. She stopped breathing twice." Then he looked at me.

"I got a car in the garage. I'm not sure I remember how to drive it."

I drove him to the hospital and waited with him. When they brought her up to the room, Mr. Uber winced. Here was his beloved: the young girl to whom he had pledged his faithfulness, and kept it all these years. His bride was now eighty-seven; they had been married for more than sixty years.

When I took Mr. Uber home that evening I wrote my name and phone number in large letters on a piece of paper and taped it next to his phone.

"I know your name," he said with bewilderment.

"I know. But you may need me during the night. You know how it is when you've been asleep. Call me anytime. If you need a ride, call me."

The call came shortly after midnight.

"The hospital called," he said.

"Yes. Do you need a ride?"

"I have to make arrangements."

Although it has been many years since we moved from that small town, sometimes I still hear that voice in the night. I saw him from time to time when we returned to visit. Mr. Uber was in his nineties then. He had traveled to California to see his daughter and hadn't liked the trip. He still sat on the stoop before his narrow house, or worked in the garden, or smoked Edgeworth from a Prince Albert tin.

In an age when marriage is under attack from within and from without, such examples of simple faithfulness as that of Mr. Uber seem increasingly rare. For years he had cared for his incapacitated wife. Lovingly he had tended to her needs. He had been faithful, and his faithfulness ended, as all things on this earth must, in her passing. But that is not really the ending. In one sense, the faithfulness lives on in the legacy such a person leaves for future generations. But in another sense, a very real sense, the ultimate consummation has just begun.

Just recently I received news that Mr. Uber, too, had died. It is a sad note, for in this life I'll not see him again. But not entirely sad, at least not if we accept the promises of Scripture. For if our earthly marriage is but a picture of Christ's faithfulness to his bride, the Church, then Mr. and Mrs. Uber are celebrating once again.

REFLECTIONS

1. Some marriage vows still contain the old phrase "I plight thee my troth," which, translated into more contemporary language, means "I pledge my faithfulness to you." What does it mean to "keep troth" in a marriage?

   How can this be done in practical ways?

   How is faithfulness the key to keeping this commandment—and *all* the commandments—as well as the key to a successful marriage?

2. Read a section of the creation account in Genesis 2:18-24. What does this passage say about the relationship between husband and wife? About marriage?

   What is the significance of the following elements in this account?

   God made a special creature to be a "suitable helper" to the man.

   The Lord created woman from the man's rib.

   When he saw the woman, the man said, "This is now bone of my bones and flesh of my flesh."

   "For this reason a man will leave his father and mother and be united to his wife, and they will become one flesh."

3. What implications does this commandment have for those people who are not married?

   How is "keeping troth" a positive guideline also for single people?

4. What seems to be the prevailing attitude toward marriage in today's world? Toward human sexuality?

How do these attitudes square off with those expressed in this commandment?

How do *you* feel about marriage and sexuality?

5. In their feelings about marriage, people often confuse subjugation, which is a kind of slavery to a dominant power, with "being subject to." How are marriage partners subject to each other in the matter of keeping faithfulness?

6. The story of Leroy Uber offers a number of wonderful illustrations of fidelity. Consider how this man's entire life reflects efforts to "keep faithfulness." How was Leroy Uber a positive influence in the author's own life and marriage?

What are some of the most prominent influences or examples for marriage partners today?

Think of an example of faithfulness from your own experience and relationships—either in or outside a marriage. List qualities that best illustrate that faithfulness.

8

Taking and Withholding

You shall not steal.

EXODUS 20:15

The delights of the teaching profession for me occur not only in the classroom but also in a place where students live and move and have their being—the coffee shop of the college commons. The atmosphere is relaxed and friendly. Sometimes I sit there alone, just enjoying the rush of noise and excitement. Sometimes others join me.

It's when I sit alone, a cup of coffee steaming before me, when I am pretending to be working on a yellow legal pad at something academic, that I make headway in my lifelong pursuit of understanding human nature. I am often really taking notes—hastily and imprecisely—on the discussions careening around me.

The Lesson of Students

One recently overheard conversation amazed me. A group of students had apparently been meeting once a week to study the Ten Commandments—of all things!—and one member of the group had tried to invite a newcomer along. The group was recalling that invitation. The comments were accompanied by a great deal of boisterous laughter and good-hearted digs, but the gist of the conversation that I recorded goes like this:

A student said: We were having early lunch and this transfer student, George, sits at our table. After we talk for a couple of minutes he leans over and says, "What do you guys do in that little room you go to after lunch?"

So I say to him, "We're studying the Ten Commandments."
George gets this dazed look on his face.

"This is true," I say. "You want to join us? You'd be welcome to join us."

"No thanks," says George. "I just don't get excited about all this religious stuff."

"Hey, you ought to try chapel some time," I suggest.

"Forced religion stinks in the nostrils of God," he says.

132

"So who's forcing you?"

"Hey, I'm religious. Don't get me wrong. Else I wouldn't be at this college. I got baptized once."

"But religion is more than baptism," I say. "I mean it is a way of life, isn't it?"

"Yeah. That's cool," says George.

I was caught by George's reply, "That's cool." I wonder if he ever joined the group. But something about that easy rejoinder, "That's cool," distanced George from the commandments altogether, as if they were some foreign thing that may have interested others but didn't necessarily apply to him. Perhaps no other commandment is so immediately applicable to everyone as this one: "You shall not steal." My guess is that, if George had wandered into the discussion group on the day this commandment was discussed, he would have immediately felt the heat of relevance breathing down the neck of "That's cool." Sooner or later, each one of us confronts this commandment in a dramatically personal way, for the commandment leaves very little "wiggle-room" to sneak away from it.

Stealing: Our Common Guilt

Some of the prior commandments may seem, at first glance, not to apply directly to us. It may be easy, for example, to say that we have not committed adultery because we are not married. But we have to rethink our position when we understand the full implications and relevance of the commandment to all areas of human sexuality and keeping faithfulness.

Likewise, the commandment about stealing has broad implications for all people in all circumstances. One extreme interpretation of the commandment is the view that theft is nothing short of armed robbery. At the other extreme lies the view that failure to do everything or anything that we *should* do constitutes a theft from service to God. In this latter view, one scarcely has time to enjoy a sunny afternoon, to relax, to enjoy life. In a way, such failure to enjoy God's gifts could also be construed as a kind of theft. Both views, however, lock us into pigeonholes wherein we lose sight of God's grace and love.

It is helpful to our understanding that, as with all God's commandments, this one may be seen in a proscriptive and a prescriptive way. It makes clear what we should *not* do, but it also implies what we *should* do. In his Small Catechism, Martin Luther expresses both sides in his explanation of the commandment: "We should fear and love God that we may not take our neighbor's money or goods, but help him to improve and protect his property and business."

The commandment reads: "You shall not steal." What is this thing called "stealing"? In its simplest terms, stealing is taking something that doesn't belong to you. Any taking of someone else's property is stealing. We recall, however, that adultery is a kind of theft in that it steals from the marriage by destroying faithfulness. Stealing now begins to broaden. It is more than actively seizing something that belongs to another; it also includes failure to give what is rightfully due.

Making Commitments/Breaking Vows

Commitments are risky things. They extend into the unknown future, promising that we won't change when, in fact, change seems to be the one certainty about the future. Yet we make commitments almost as casually as we breathe. We sign contracts for everything from charge cards to car loans to home mortgages. We make arrangements to have lunch together and also to have a lifetime together. Our society is intricately knit together by countless ties of commitment.

Is it any wonder that our commitments break down? Who can possibly keep them all? And anytime they break down, from the most minor to the most monumental commitment—from a broken prom date to a banking scandal—

pain occurs. We feel violated by infidelity. Breaking commitments is a theft of a trust.

Sometimes our broken commitments are caused by mere oversights or forgetfulness. It is not that we actively break a promise, turning our back upon it, but rather that we let the commitment diminish in priority, ignore it, and let it finally dwindle to nothing. One concrete example might guide our reflection here. It is a painful one for me, for it exposes one of my own shortcomings.

I believe that prayer is the lifeblood of a Christian's relationship with God; it is the difference between a living relationship and a dead one. So I commit myself to regular, daily prayer time, first thing in the morning before the events of a busy day begin to drain my energy and divert my attention. Part of that prayer time consists of intercession for my family, for the concerns of my support group members, and for other needs.

When our church started a prayer support ministry for its high school and college students, I gladly accepted an assignment. I prayed devotedly for my young partner—in virtual anonymity—for several months. But as time lapsed, so did my attention. By the end of the year, I thought of my partner's name with more guilt than support.

I learned something about myself through that. I learned the weaknesses of my own commitments, and how very easy it is to let them slide into the pool of forgetfulness. I also learned that I need very specific events and a very specific time frame for my prayer life. Now when I tell someone I'll pray for her or him, I specify that it will be for one week. And I do that. We have to frame our commitments in terms of what we can actually and realistically do.

Commission and Omission

Theft can slip into our lives through the things we do and the things we fail to do—through commission and omission.

Sins of commission are those actively engaged. Sins of omission are those things we *ought* to do but fail to do. One student, for example, may commit the theft of plagiarism—stealing someone else's ideas or words—in order to get a good grade on a term paper. Another student may simply not bother to write the required term paper. The consequence in both cases will likely be an "F." Both actions carry a penalty, because both are forms of stealing—one of someone else's work, the other of the responsibility to do one's own work. In the latter case, one has stolen from one's own obligations, or responsibilities.

There are all kinds of temptations to what we might call "active" theft—the sin of commission: cheating on income taxes, taking a book left behind in a classroom, underpaying a worker for the worth of his performance, fixing a basketball game, or setting a loan at an exorbitant interest rate. But there are probably even more temptations to steal by omission—failing to fulfill our responsibilities, neglecting to use our time wisely, ignoring the rights, needs, and well-being of others.

The familiar parable that Jesus told about the Prodigal Son could be understood in this context. There was a young man who took his inheritance early and then just took off, seeking a life of pleasure and good times—until his money ran out. The son didn't steal from others, but he did squander all the responsibilities and gifts that he had been given by his father. This was theft.

How We Steal from God

Yet a third example has to do with how we use the gifts God has given to us. If God has given us talents or gifts and we refuse to use them, we are ultimately robbing God. We withhold from God his due or what he requires of us. God requires, for example, that we use our gifts, live in harmony with others, help the poor and needy. Failure to do these things is just as much a form of stealing as failure to pay income tax—that amount due the government as your responsibility as a citizen. The citizen of the kingdom of God can do no less with God's requirements.

While being citizens of God's kingdom includes certain spiritual responsibilities due God, it also includes financial responsibilities. Tithing is the one financial responsibility God has given us. Failure to tithe is treated in the Bible as a kind of theft.

It may be difficult to understand why tithing is so important. God doesn't need our money, after all. The Bible says that God owns the cattle on a thousand hills; he owns the hills, too. But precisely because of that, tithing is important. If God owns all things, whatever we have comes from him. All God asks in return—not because he *needs* it, but as a sign of our gratitude and faithfulness—is a tithe.

Probably the first tithe-giving recorded in the Bible was when Abraham gave King Melchizedek one-tenth of all his goods. But notice the reason. Melchizedek says, in Genesis 14:19, "Blessed be Abram by God Most High, maker of heaven and earth; and blessed be God Most High, who has delivered your enemies into your hand!" Abraham's tithe was a response to God's goodness. The Pentateuch, the first five books of the Bible, over and over again emphasizes the importance of tithing, always to be given as "firstfruits," before we attend to other necessities. And God holds the people to this requirement. Very directly he says that withholding tithes is robbing God. In his Old Testament prophecies, Malachi called his people back to God. He was a spokesman for God, who longed to have his people reunited in a loving relationship with God. But the people, so far out of step with that relationship, wondered how. Malachi responds like this:

"[R]eturn to me, and I will return to you," says the Lord Almighty. But you ask, "How are we to return?" Will a man rob God? Yet you are robbing me. But you say, "How are we robbing thee?" In your tithes and offerings. You are under a curse—the whole nation of you—because you are robbing

*me. Bring the whole tithes into the storehouse, that there may
be food in my house. Test me in this, says the Lord Almighty,
and see if I will not throw open the windows of heaven and
pour out so much blessing (Malachi 3:7-10).*

Notice the wonderful promise of blessing that God offers
to those who faithfully tithe. Here we begin to see the positive counterpart of this commandment.

Stewardship of the Earth

One final practical application of this commandment can
apply to our stewardship of God's earth. Warnings about the
need to care for our planet proliferate daily; so too do the
effects of failure to heed those warnings. Yet many Christians—those who should be foremost in the battle to care for
God's earth—still ignore these warnings. We go about our
lives, perhaps listening, but doing nothing.

We do well to pause and reflect upon this world that God
has shaped and formed with such intricate care and such
heart-rending beauty. Study the shimmering curtain of clouds
against a high blue sky. Enjoy the delicate blossoms against a
field of green. Feel the cold bite of a January wind, edged
with flakes of snow that coat the mountains, that replenish
the streams and rivers.

This earth is dying down and running out. It is not
enough, never enough, for Christians passively to accept
God's gift. Our task is to treasure and nurture it. And we
are to protect it, as the prophet Jeremiah pointed out:
"What man is wise enough to understand this? Who has been
instructed by the Lord and can explain it? Why has the land
been ruined and laid waste like a desert that no one can
cross?" (Jeremiah 9:12). Every bit of litter, every bit of garbage
that could be composted or recycled, is an act of theft against
this beauty that God has given to all of us. We have to fall in
love all over again with God's creation, to try to glimpse

through the despoiling of the air, the land, and the waters, a bit of Eden.

The Positive Counterpart

As with each of God's commandments, this one warns us against wrongdoing, against any behavior that threatens our close relationship with God. But it also has a positive side that deepens that relationship. If stealing is taking from someone what is not rightfully ours, or if it is taking from what we should rightfully do, then the positive counterpart lies in *giving*—to others and to God. The ultimate model of a life of giving comes from Jesus. Consider four gifts Jesus has given us, and how they, in turn, can empower us to bring those gifts to others.

His Life

Put aside notions of Christmas pageants and manger scenes and think back to God's appearance in lightning and thunder on Sinai. The people fell to the ground in terror. This God of all creation set foot on his creation, and it shook beneath him. It was too small to hold even a glimpse of his glory.

But in his greatest gift to us, this Maker God made *himself* small enough for creation to contain him. He became tiny so that he could be born before humans who could see him, touch him, hear him.

The mighty God became small in order to draw near to us.

And herein God provides us a practical, concrete guideline for giving. We, too, can give by drawing near to others. We don't stand apart, inaccessible and remote. Sometimes we have to become very small in order to hear the whispers of pain that would otherwise pass us by. We give of ourselves, rather than taking from others.

His Death

When I reflect upon Jesus' life, it amazes me how brief it actually was. Even in a historical period when the expected life span was far shorter than ours, his life was cut tragically short. Yet look what he did in those brief years. He healed the sick, brought peace to broken hearts, saved the lost by forgiving their sins. One would wish his life would go on for years, cutting an ever-larger swath through history.

But Jesus was born to die. He was born to be an *atonement*, that we—at any time in history—might be made right with God.

We don't often think in terms of atonement nowadays. We think instead of what we owe. That is, if I run up an account on my credit card, *I* have to pay it off—and with interest. Now imagine that my debts are so large I'm facing bankruptcy. Suppose someone pays it all for me. That is an example of atonement. But Jesus' atonement is far, far more radical, because here one person stands in place of us, takes all our sins—our debts to God—upon himself, and makes us completely new. We are a new creation, freed in Christ.

The tragedy of Jesus' death is a victory for us. It also guides us in practical Christian living. Jesus' atonement frees us for sacrificial living. We put our trust and our hope in one who has redeemed us through his atoning death; our hope is not in this world. Therefore, we are free to give and live sacrificially, freed especially from the anxieties of this world which tell us to *get* as much as we can as quickly as we can. And Jesus' atonement also frees us to tell the good news of his freedom to others. If we know—with the rock-solid assurance of Jesus' own promises—that we are free, we can bring this gift to others with confidence.

His Resurrection

Too often we end a study of Jesus' life with the crucifixion. But the crucifixion was certainly not the end for him; and it is not for us. By his resurrection Jesus opened the door to heaven for us, and he also promised that we will be together with him always. Here is a gift we long for; and yet it is also a gift *we already have*. The promise of resurrection is already ours, as Paul wrote to the Christians in Rome that nothing will be able to separate us from the love of God in Christ Jesus our Lord (Romans 8:39).

This is a gift that we cannot hoard for ourselves, like some collection of precious coins. Give it away! Share it with others. It offers the hope people need of a full life now, and a life that never ends.

His Great Commission

Jesus came into this world—God made himself small—to draw close to us. He bent down to his children's height. Jesus died, atoning for the sins of these children. He was placed in a dark tomb, a stone was rolled across its entrance, his corpse was sealed within. Jesus arose from that grave; he arose from the bonds of death itself, giving his people the gift of life everlasting.

Such rich gifts. And Jesus had one more. He told us what to do with the wonderful gifts he gives us: *give them away.*

After Jesus was crucified, his disciples scattered in fear and confusion. Only the brave women who supported his earthly ministry supported him to the end. After Jesus' death, the disciples went into hiding. But the women who loved Jesus went to his tomb, hoping to anoint his body. Mary Magdalene was there to see her resurrected Lord. And the first thing she did was to run out and *tell someone,* in this case the fearful disciples. When Jesus later appeared to the disciples, "he rebuked them for their lack of faith and their stubborn refusal to believe those who had seen him after he had risen" (Mark 16:14). Following that rebuke, he gave them a commission, an assignment: "Go into all the world and preach the good news to all creation. Whoever believes and is baptized will be saved, but whoever does not believe will be condemned" (Mark 16:15-16).

We are mistaken if we think of the commission as an onerous, heavy duty. We don't need a Mack truck to carry the gospel to others. A joyful, grateful heart works far better than a Mack truck. And we are equally mistaken if we think going "to all creation" excludes the world of our own block. We are on commission for Christ in each day and each place that he gives us.

Balancing the Commandment

The commandment against stealing has enormous scope. Its proscriptive side—"You shall not steal"—might seem clear enough. But we also see that it extends into some unexpected areas: making commitments and breaking vows, sins of commission and omission, our use of God-given gifts, and our stewardship of God's creation.

Faithfulness to this commandment is also a matter of balance. If we try to avoid those sins of omission, especially, it is possible to let a host of responsibilities overwhelm our lives. I have known people who are not just weary in well-doing, but have plain worn out. They grow depressed and exhausted trying to right every evil, meet every need. A marvelously practical guideline for keeping things in balance lies in assessing the gifts and talents God has given each of us. If God calls us to service in his kingdom, he also endows us with unique gifts by which to exercise that service. Our first task is to discover those gifts by which we are best suited to meet God's calling.

As we keep faithfulness to God, we understand the liberation of each commandment. We are freed to serve God according to the gifts and tasks he has given us. If theft is the negative act, then joyful service is the positive counterpart to this commandment against stealing. Instead of taking, we live a life of giving—in thanksgiving for the gifts God has so richly bestowed.

REFLECTIONS

1. This chapter opens the understanding of "stealing" to include an enormous range of things: actually committing armed robbery, breaking vows, failure to use our God-given gifts, failure to help others, failure to tithe. How can each of these be a form of theft?

Is this broad understanding one that is shared by our society? What seems to be the popular cultural attitude toward stealing? Describe some evidences of this attitude.

2. How do *you* define "stealing"?

Think about instances when you have broken this commandment. If you were to rank your sins of stealing, which would you label "serious" sins? What makes those more serious than others violations of the commandment?

What was behind your impulse to steal?

3. Under the section **How We Steal from God,** the author talks about tithing and failure to tithe. In the biblical understanding of this term, a tithe is an offering of a tenth of our possessions, always to be given as "first-fruits," before we attend to other necessities. Farmers were to select the choicest offerings from the first crop and offer it to God.

How is the idea of "firstfruits" important to the concept of tithing? Why was it important that the offering to God be taken from the best and the first of our earnings?

What does such an offering do for the one who gives it?

Do you think God expects us to give one-tenth of our "firstfruits" today? How would you define "one-tenth" and "firstfruits"? What are some concrete ways this could be done?

4. The chapter suggests that failure to tithe and failure to take care of our earth are both sins against this commandment. In what sense are such failures sins?

Do you agree? Are such sins as serious as, say, armed robbery?

5. The Ten Commandments warn us against sins—against deliberate turning away from God. We usually think of such acts as murder or stealing as *crimes*, as violations of someone else's rights. We don't often use the term "sin" in referring to them. But they are also sins against God— sins that turn away from God and damage our relationship with God.

How is the act of stealing from another person a sin against—a theft from—God?

6. Each commandment has a negative and a positive thrust—telling us what we should not do and implying what we should do. If "stealing" is the negative, forbidden, act in this commandment, how is *giving* its positive counterpart?

The author suggests that, if we truly want to keep this commandment, we need to "draw near to others" and to "become very small." How might each of those suggestions help us keep the commandment against stealing?

9

Telling the Truth

You shall not give false testimony

against your neighbor.

EXODUS 20:15

If we had only one commandment instead of ten, which one should it be? Obviously, it would have to be the first one, "I am the Lord your God, who brought you out of the land of Egypt, out of the house of bondage. You shall have no other gods before me." All the others apply this commandment by exposing the idols we place before God. Lying, stealing, adultery, disobedience to parents, covetousness—all make gods of our own desires and turn us away from worship of the true God.

The challenge of the commandment against giving "false testimony against your neighbor," or as the Revised Standard Version of the Bible puts it, "false witness against your neighbor," fits into the pattern. To understand the full implications of this commandment, we must consider what is meant by "false witness" or "false testimony," and *who* is meant by "your neighbor."

Who Is Your Neighbor?

Remember that in this second table of the law, God tells us how to live with others—our family and our neighbors. In his parable of the good Samaritan, Jesus taught that our neighbor is anyone we come into contact with, anyone who is in need—whether that person is like us or unlike us, beautiful or unlovely, sick or well.

To us, the word *neighbor* usually means someone close by, those with whom we live in daily contact. We speak of "our neighborhood" and "our neighbors" to signify a community. The radical nature of Jesus' teaching breaks these walls of comfortable relationships. He shoves us out into an uncomfortable *world* of relationships, which include people with whom we might not choose to have relationships.

The Lesson of Charles

I didn't want to be a neighbor to Charles. He was huge and ugly—a mean kind of ugly. His eyes bore wounds and

146

anger and a seething pain. Besides that, he had just been released from prison the morning I met him. He flashed his release form in my face while asking for money to stay at the YMCA.

Ironically, my neighbor up the block had sent him to me. My neighbor knew I was a "church person." He wanted to get rid of Charles, so he sent him to me. Now I wanted to get rid of Charles. He was too big, too frightening, to be standing in my yard. To be my neighbor.

"Your neighbor said you'd give me money," he said. "I just got out of prison. I gotta make a new start."

Charles was looking angry. "I got a short temper," he said. "It's been my trouble."

"Listen, Charles," I said. "I'll take you down to the mission. They'll give you the help you need."

"Can't go to no mission," he exploded.

"Why's that, Charles?"

"I can't never go back there. Judge said that."

"Oh?"

"That's where I killed the man I got sent to prison for."

My wife, meanwhile, was preparing a plateful of dinner for Charles. She called him over to the porch. A heaping platter of ham and potatoes that Charles shoveled down like a starving man. It calmed him. Two huge glasses of milk cooled him off.

"Listen," I said. "I'll drive you to the YMCA. I'll write you a check for a week's stay. Okay?"

"I really want to go to Ruby's house," he said. "She's taking care of my children. I want to see them."

"Where's your wife?" my wife asked.

"In prison," Charles said.

I took Charles to Ruby's house, a run-down place, on one of the poorest streets of the city. He thanked me heartily. People turned and stared at this white face that was as out of place in their neighborhood as Charles had been in my back yard. He asked me to thank my wife for the dinner and the twenty-dollar bill she had slipped him. He said he might be in our church Sunday, he was so happy.

When I arrived back home from Ruby's place, my wife murmured, "Sometimes you entertain angels unawares." One thing I learned from this experience with Charles: I won't see him in our church. The follow-up contacts for work or help that I gave him proved, upon my checking, not to have been followed up.

Lesson number two from Charles: I don't know what happened to him because *I* failed to follow up also. I was not afraid of this big, angry man, but I wasn't comfortable with him. I certainly didn't go an extra mile. There was more I could have done. Love for neighbors, after all, isn't just a quick handout. It's entering into the life and the need of the neighbor.

Our neighbor may be anyone we meet, anyone whom God puts in our way. Sometimes we find it easy to send aid to the "neighbor" in Outer Patagonia, but very hard to go and visit the needy one a few blocks away. God requires this, however. The task of being a neighbor is just that: to show love and mercy to anyone in need. These qualifications become relevant as we attempt to define "false witness," this action toward the one who is our neighbor.

The Meaning of "False Witness"

If we defined "false witness" as an action, we would probably immediately think of lying. Lying is one way of bearing false witness, to be sure. But false witness in dealing with our neighbor can also be understood as a failure to act in love and mercy. Acting in love and mercy is the positive good; anything contrary to that is bearing false witness. Whenever we fail to act in love and mercy, we are not "witnessing," or representing ourselves truthfully as Christians to others. We can bear false witness in a number of ways.

Lying as Deception

Lying almost always bears the intention to deceive. The lying person wants, deliberately and usually for personal profit or protection, to deceive others. He or she constructs the lie to do so. This is different from an error of judgment or lack of information. Just as courts make a distinction between murder—the willful, premeditated taking of someone's life—and negligent homicide—the taking of someone's life in an accident—lying has to be understood as a deliberate act.

Several years ago, a local business owner and a member of a nearby congregation discovered that his accountant had been embezzling money from his firm. This had been going on for years, and it amounted to almost a quarter of a million dollars. The owner had trusted this accountant for years. They went to the same church and had served as elders together. The accountant had been paid a good salary and was, in fact, vice-president of finance for the company.

The accountant also had a serious addiction to gambling. It started with small bets, then escalated as he tried to cover his losses. His embezzlement was more than just theft. It involved deceit, which touched everything and everyone in his life. His embezzlement was a form of lying—and it caused clear injury to a neighbor.

It was also a crime punishable by law.

That fact caused agony for the business owner. He knew that crime has to be punished as an example to others and to uphold the principle of the law. Christians believe, after all, that God has instituted the state and its laws precisely for such circumstances. But the business owner was reluctant to prosecute his employee. He agonized over the situation for days.

His dilemma was this. This man had been a brilliant accountant. (A cynic might observe that he must have been brilliant to get away with embezzlement all those years.) The owner struggled over whether it was right to take from the man the opportunity to make restoration and to use those talents again to glorify God. Also, the owner was mindful of how prosecuting the accountant would devastate his family. Sin always affects more than the individual who sins; its consequences touch many others, as well. If the accountant faced financial ruin, so did his family. And, most important, the owner reasoned that the man was a brother in the Lord—one who had gone wrong, to be sure. But still a brother.

The owner took seriously Jesus' example of love and forgiveness and decided to try to act according to those precepts as far as he could. But he also took the Ten Commandments seriously. He demonstrated, in fact, the positive counterpart to this commandment by the way in which he dealt with this sin of false witness and theft.

First of all, in the company of another person from the firm whom he had taken into confidence, he confronted the accountant with his discovery of the embezzlement. There was no room for denials. Then they held a council with the pastor and several elders from their church: a sin had been committed. The accountant confessed his sin and asked forgiveness, no matter what the consequences. He had wanted to unburden himself, to confess, for a long time, but he didn't know how to go about it. His whole story came out: a quarter of a million dollars had been lost at race tracks, ball games, and with numbers runners.

The owner decided to give him a six-month leave of absence for intensive psychotherapy. Company insurance paid for most of this treatment. After the treatment, he reinstated the accountant in his job. But twenty-five percent of the man's salary went to repaying the debt.

The story has a happy ending. The accountant did not escape the consequences of his crime, but he is productive once again—in a positive way. He has been forgiven. He has hopes for repaying his debt. He can retain some sense of honor.

Perhaps honor is the key to this commandment also. Any lying, any bearing of false witness, injures a neighbor's honor. The positive counterpart is to honor your neighbor, looking out for that neighbor's good before your own.

Lying as Gossip

Perhaps one of the most common and most harmful ways of bearing false witness is through gossip. Like gambling, gossip can become a compulsion. It satisfies a human need for attention, but at the cost of someone else's honor.

Exodus 23:1 speaks strongly to the sin of gossip: "Do not spread false reports. Do not help a wicked man by being a malicious witness." Gossip steals from the neighbor's reputation or honor, and it appears in so many different forms. We commonly understand gossip as "saying bad things" about someone, but surely it also includes *listening* to the gossip of others. We become willing participants in the deed by listening to malicious words. Consider also that gossip can involve telling *truths* that are harmful to a person's reputation: stories out of a person's past—sins confessed and forgiven—that are heaped anew on that person's head. Aren't we pretending to be better than God in those cases, since God himself has promised forgiveness?

Gossip is one of the saddest of sins: it is a veritable cry from one's own weak self-image. The gossiper collects and spreads information about others because of a desperate need for attention. I don't think it's ever a case of some people just having a "big mouth." There's something intrinsically wrong with the person who gossips. And that wrongness has to be corrected by a new sense of self-worth through Christ. The person who gossips needs a healed heart and a healed tongue.

A friend once observed to me that gossip could be stopped in its tracks simply by repeating the following words when the temptation arises: "Jesus loves me. Jesus died for me." This is a reminder of our worth that should eliminate the need to speak ill of others. Then we can focus on the positive counterpart of gossip, replacing it with *good* words about our neighbor, words that will build him or her up.

In this commandment we see again how beautifully practical God's laws are. Gossip damages not only the person on its receiving end, but also the gossiper—by turning that person's world into a narrow, ugly realm of malicious talk. Conversely, the person who builds up others also builds up himself or herself. It is not just spiritual reality; it is also a psychological one. When we encourage others, when we speak well of them, we improve our relations with them and with anyone who hears us. And we grow closer to the God who loves us and our neighbor.

The Value of Truth

We have explored various manifestations of bearing "false witness" and seen how these sins can damage us and our neighbor. Now it is time to focus on the heart of this commandment. Did God warn us against lying simply because it's a good social thing to avoid injuring one's neighbor with hurtful words? Rather, the commandment evidences the fact that *truth* is the highest value in the life of God's people.

We are to live lives of truth, first of all, because God is truth. Jeremiah 10:10 states that the Lord is the true God, and he is the *true* God in a nation of idol-worshipers. Jesus also accepts this claim when, in John 14:6, he says, "I am the way and the truth and the life." Lies cannot stand in the presence of God. The importance of truthful living is spelled out in the New Testament letter that John wrote to followers of Jesus: "I do not write to you because you do not know the truth, but because you do know it and because no lie comes from the truth. Who is the liar? It is the man who denies that Jesus is the Christ. Such a man is the antichrist—he denies the Father and the Son" (1 John 2: 21-22). Just as all truth comes from God, so all lies come from Satan, who is called the "father of lies." This commandment isn't only a guide to good social behavior.

The commandment against lying invokes the whole spiritual warfare between God and Satan, between truth and lies, between life and death. That's why God promises such rich blessing for truthfulness. In Psalm 15, David begins by asking: "Lord, who may dwell in your sanctuary? Who may live on your holy hill?" Verses 2 and 3 answer: "He whose walk is blameless and who does what is righteous, who speaks the truth from his heart and has no slander on his tongue, who does his neighbor no wrong and casts no slur on his fellow man." Telling the truth—living the truth—enacts God's love in and for this world. It testifies to the divine harmony, nurturing, and well-being he wills for all people.

How to Speak Truthfully

As with all the commandments, there is implicit in the warning a loving guide; behind the law against lying lies its positive counterpart—rules for truthful living. Perhaps the first one emerges from my vocation as an English teacher, but I believe it holds for all of us—that is, truthfulness of language. To avoid lying, to speak truthfully, we do not distort things; we choose our words with care; we also *listen* —lovingly and carefully—in order to know which words to choose. Moreover, truthfulness in language suggests that we keep our word. We don't promise more than we can keep. Here, as in all the other commandments, fidelity is our guide to right behavior.

Finally, too, we follow truthful living by the way we represent Christ to others in our words and actions. This point has implications for how we evangelize others. Some evangelistic television programs try to attract people by painting a picture of Christianity that bears little relationship to human reality, and by treating the person being evangelized as no more than a customer needing a product. Here the impact of the commandment, with its emphasis on truthfulness and love of neighbor, speaks clearly. It also gives us directions to bear in mind in any evangelism program. True evangelism entails responsibilities and commitments. It begins in a commitment that is something like friendship.

One might say that love is the ultimate goal of true friendship. But love is the *first step* in evangelism. We reach out to others not because we feel comfortable with them, nor because we hold interests in common, but because of Jesus' love for them. And that love extends to the unlovely and unloving, people who especially need to learn of Jesus' love through us.

But when we explore this image of evangelism as friendship, we see a much larger picture. It isn't just *our* friendship we extend as we present the truth of God to others, it is an invitation to them to be friends with God himself.

Satan would love to have us forsake the world to him, to have us live and interact only with other Christians. Such living is a false witness, for it is no witness at all. We have a responsibility to redeem and reclaim the world. Jesus' words can chart the course for lives of witness to the truth: "I have not come to call the righteous, but sinners" (Luke 5:32). We can do no less. In all our actions and words of truth, in all our deeds of compassion and love, we model Jesus to the world.

Lying and *loving* differ only by three letters, yet they are polar opposites. Through Jesus, our lives can change from ones of lying to ones of loving. At the end of the change comes the discovery also of truly *living* in the presence of Christ.

REFLECTIONS

1. This commandment is about telling the truth. In fact, it's about *living* the truth. It's not easy to define "truth," but it is extremely important for our lives and for our relationships with God and others. Try it: How would you define truth?

2. Several times in the chapter, the author makes the point that God puts such strong emphasis on truth-telling because God is truth. What does it mean that "God is truth"?

   If you turn that statement around, it might be easier to handle: Truth is God. How would you explain that idea?

3. If God is truth, then everything that is of God is true and real; and anything that is *not* of God is false. Satan is often called "the father of lies" because he wants to turn us away from God's truth and live in a world that is not focused on God—a world of lies.

   In what sense are we living a lie—"bearing false witness"—whenever we disobey God?

4. Think about your own experiences with lies, about lies that you have told, and about lies told about you. What happens when someone lies?

   How does lying affect human relationships?

   How does it affect the person who tells the lies?

5. The story about the business owner and the embezzler offers several surprising understandings that relate to this

commandment. In what sense was the embezzler bearing false witness as well as stealing?

Do you think his employer's solution was appropriate? What action might you have taken in his place?

6. Christians often discuss ways in which they can witness to their faith or to their God. What do they mean by "witness" in such conversations?

What are the most effective ways of witnessing to our faith?

How is "bearing false witness against our neighbor" also bearing false witness against God?

10

Learning to Be Satisfied

You shall not covet your neighbor's house.

You shall not covet your neighbor's wife,

or his manservant or maidservant,

his ox or donkey, or anything that belongs

to your neighbor.

EXODUS 20:17

The treatment of this verse represents a second divergence in the way different traditions align the Ten Commandments. We recall that the first occasion was the division of the first and second commandments. The verse about coveting has been separated by Catholic, Episcopalian, and Lutheran traditions into the ninth and tenth commandments—"You shall not covet your neighbor's house" and "You shall not covet your neighbor's wife, or his manservant or maidservant, his ox or donkey, or anything that belongs to your neighbor." Other traditions of the Christian faith view the verse as one commandment against coveting. It is important to note, however, that even though Martin Luther divided the verse into two commandments in his Large Catechism, he discusses them jointly.

What is the common thread among the stipulations in this verse? And how does it relate to the whole body of God's law? The warning in verse 17 is against coveting—a desire that arises from deep in one's heart. The problem is that coveting is a desire for something that doesn't belong to us. Here is the pattern we have observed in all the commandments: a longing for something that can satisfy our yearnings and desires. And, as was true in the other commandments, that longing may be turned toward things of this world or toward God. Coveting is when we turn our longings toward worldly things.

Perhaps a story can shed some light on this human longing. It's an innocent story about a child's powerful longing for candy. But there are lessons to be learned from the story. I was the child, and my story is about "Uncle Bert's Candy Store."

Cassopolis, Michigan, is a little dot of a town dropped alongside a bend in the road. It holds a couple of old mills and dilapidated gas stations, some leaning storefronts, and narrow little houses scattered about. Driving through Cassopolis on the crooked road, one barely notices that it is a town.

My Uncle Bert, a big, dark-haired man, full of humor and energy, came with his wife, Dorothy, and three children to pastor a church in Cassopolis. The church was a hodge-podge of denominational allegiances. Part southern Baptist and part northern Presbyterian, the church simply called itself "United Presbyterian" and called my Uncle Albertus Groen-dyk to pastor it.

United Presbyterian was long on dreams and short on cash. It didn't pay its pastor much. But Uncle Bert, like tent-maker Paul, found his own means to help support his family. He started a candy business, supplying out of his home a line of vending machines.

I hungered after candy in those years. My sweet tooth was my whole body. I annihilated candy bars, sweet mints, gumballs. And my Uncle Bert was a candy dealer.

When I remember him now, I often picture Uncle Bert in his study, boxes of candy rising around his desk and piled on top of theological texts. Boxes of gumballs stood brightly colored like ornaments. Candy bars of all kinds. My recollections of Uncle Bert are indelibly mixed with those mountains of candy.

At Christmas, our family squeezed into the old Ford and went to visit Uncle Bert and Aunt Dorothy in Cassopolis. It was an annual pilgrimage, and my hunger was stirred by the expectation of sweet joy at a feast of candy.

Now, there are two ways to keep a candy store. One way is to recognize this longing that burns in children and to lock the candy away. The other was Uncle Bert's way. He recognized this hunger for candy that burned in me, but he was a giver.

The day before Christmas we arrived at the Groendyk house. We frolicked with cousins and their electric train. We grew weary with wonder before the Christmas tree. And then Uncle Bert would catch my eye. His big hand found my small shoulder, and he led me to the study. He told me to help myself, sweeping his hand across the room. Help myself! Then, after I had taken as much as I dared, he told me to take more. My hands weren't full enough, he said. Here's some for your pockets on the way home.

I confess that I have never outgrown those memories. Uncle Bert stands forever in my mind, hand on my young shoulders, holding the door open to his "candy room."

Less than a month after we returned home from one Christmas in Cassopolis, Uncle Bert died of a heart attack. It happened two days before my tenth birthday. A child does not forget these things. When he died, Uncle Bert was one year younger than I now am as I write this. Yet, somehow, I am still that little boy, awestruck as I feel that hand on my thin shoulders. Help yourself. It's all yours.

As an adult, I now understand the full implications of that desire that burned in me at such an early age. I think, when I reflect upon it, that my longing for God is met in a way like Uncle Bert's way of satisfying my craving for candy. God always gives beyond my expectations, sometimes in surprising ways.

Another lesson emerges from Uncle Bert's Candy Store. I most certainly enjoyed that candy while I had it—but it disappeared awfully quickly, leaving me feeling a lot worse than when I was devouring it. And it wasn't long before the old craving returned once again.

Like children's craving for candy, our human desires can never be fully satisfied. That is the tragedy of coveting: each new possession longed for is immediately superseded by new longing, and none of those longings can ever be satisfied.

When we covet, we are longing for all the wrong things. What is the root of this human longing?

Fallen Humanity

We should remind ourselves that God's commandments begin by addressing fallen human nature. In most basic terms, the Law of God defines right and wrong for people who don't always know the difference. Having been given free choice, humans often choose the bad thing, so God gave them directions for choosing the right, the good, thing.

Because he loves us and holds each of us worthy, God gave us complete freedom to love him back. God did not create automatons, within whom he programmed a circuit for love so that he could get instant love upon the flip of a switch. We are free to *choose* whether or not we will love God.

When humanity made the wrong choice—and this began in Eden, by deciding to follow self-interest and self-love rather than God—human nature changed entirely. We are still God's creation, and therefore worthy—worthy enough for Jesus to come to this world and die on the cross for our wrong choices. But because of our fallen nature, our inclination to turn away from God's love, we are incapable by our own power of choosing the right thing. We need God's power and God's guidance.

In a sense, we arrive at the end of this study back where we began. We observed at the outset that God gave the commandments because he loves us and wants us to stay in close communion with him. We have seen how the commandments are a road map that takes us back to God. They provide directions by which we set our hearts toward the goal of a loving relationship with God, a goal that puts God first in our lives.

The commands about coveting go right to the heart of God's law—to *our* heart—and force us to look once again at what we hold most dear.

What Does It Mean to Covet?

We commonly define coveting simply as wishing something that belongs to someone else were ours. Theft would be the actual taking; coveting is the desire of the heart. The commandment specifies some things that one might covet—a neighbor's house, another person's wife, or his property—called here his ox or his donkey, but we might call them his Porsche or his snowblower. To understand coveting fully, however, we have to turn away from the objects for a moment to the person who covets.

Covetous people are dissatisfied people—discontent with what they have, always looking for something more. They tend to compare themselves with people who have *more*, rather than less, and therefore are never happy. Coveting, it would seem, is an internal matter, a matter of the heart. Why, then, is this commandment included in the second table of the law, which deals with our relations to our neighbor? Murder kills someone, after all. Stealing deprives someone else of something rightfully belonging to him or her. Adultery involves another party. Bad thoughts? What's so bad about them? Do they really harm anyone else?

The Gospel of Mark records a scene where a Jewish scribe, one who knew the commandments well and kept careful track of them, approached Jesus to ask which is the greatest commandment, the one that summarizes all others. Jesus quotes from two passages in the Old Testament books of Deuteronomy and Leviticus when he answers:

> *The most important one . . . is this: "Hear, O Israel, the Lord our God, the Lord is one. Love the Lord your God with all your heart and with all your soul and with all your mind and with all your strength." The second is this: "Love your neighbor as yourself." There is no commandment greater than these (Mark 12:29-31).*

Certainly we shouldn't commit murder against our neighbor. Indeed, we shouldn't steal from our neighbor. But in his answer to the scribe, Jesus tells us what *attitude* to have toward our neighbors, how to *feel* about them. Any coveting, any envy, any discontented desire, disrupts the harmony of our relation with our neighbors. If I covet someone's property or gifts, I can't really love that person.

Coveting and *envy* are often used interchangeably to convey the thrust of this commandment. They are similar, both actions of a fallen heart.

The fundamental question underlying this commandment is "What do we *desire?*" That action of the heart is why this last commandment, together with the first, are sometimes described as bookends to all the others. Both have to do with where we direct our heart's desire; all the other commandments deal with actions that stem from that desire. At the beginning of the commandments God announces his desire for a loving relationship with us: "I am the Lord *your* God . . ." Here at the conclusion we confront our own desire for a loving relationship with God. Will I covet the things of this world, and envy others the things I don't have, or will I turn all my desire to the Lord?

Coveting is a perversion of that desire; we desire for our own sake, for our own gain. To put it simply: coveting is loving ourselves before God or neighbor. Our selfish desires dictate our thoughts and actions toward others and toward God.

Desire and the Object of Faith

For a good many years now, I have been a member of a small group of men that meets once a week for the purposes of knowing the will of God in our lives and supporting each other in efforts to grow in that knowledge. Over the years the composition of the group has shifted slightly, as old members move from the area or new ones enter and join us. Our number has ranged from four to eight members—a small group. Always the fundamental purposes have remained the same.

We try to learn God's will by studying books of the Bible and books by Christian authors. We try to support each other by keeping detailed prayer lists and committing ourselves to pray over one another's needs during the week.

Recently our group decided to study one work offered by each person that had been most influential in shaping his Christian life. The responses were varied, as different as our varied personalities. Even so, I hesitated with my own offering.

Søren Kierkegaard (1813-1855), that strange man with the strange name, is an author whom we should perhaps rediscover.

Raised in a rigidly intellectual system of the Danish Lutheran Church, Kierkegaard felt religion tightening like a noose about him. He tried to shake it off by worldly living, indulging everything his heart coveted. Turning to his own desires, he slipped further into despair, a despair haunted by the certain knowledge that he had sinned against God. One of Kierkegaard's late meditations is entitled *Purity of Heart.* In this meditation, he explains how he finally discovered that purity of heart is to desire and will one thing: the heart of God. He recognized that he had to redirect his heart from covetous desire to a longing for God.

Kierkegaard was led by God to battle his way out of despair by writing about the quest for that heart of God. One of his earliest efforts was *Fear and Trembling,* the book I selected as the most influential upon my own religious pilgrimage. It is a book I keep returning to, keep rereading, keep discovering new truths in.

In *Fear and Trembling,* Kierkegaard tries to understand the faith of Abraham in order to understand his own. What he learns is something of a surprise to him. Faith is not a matter of religious ceremonies, ethical values, or political practices.

It is a matter of the heart, seeking the Lord and desiring a relationship with him. Faith, Kierkegaard discovers, is a mystery, not fully comprehensible to the rational mind but requiring a radical commitment to a relationship with God. Sometimes this is called Kierkegaard's "leap of faith," because one is never certain of the outcome of faith until one acts on it. In faith, the desire of the heart is focused wholly on the mystery of God. How different from coveting, where the object is clearly before us.

In Abraham's life, as Kierkegaard discovered, God's will didn't always make immediate sense: "Take Isaac, thine only son, whom thou lovest, and get thee into the Land of Moriah, and offer him there . . ." But Abraham acted in faith. And the results of that faith were staggering in their rewards.

Coveting never results in satisfaction, not even if we get the thing we covet. Soon we turn our sights on something else, begin to long for yet another thing. Desire of the heart when it becomes a passion for God can satisfy forever. A passionate desire to know God, to put him first, will become ever more full and rich the further along we go.

Herein lies the enormous contrast between covetous desires and the desire of faith. Covetousness turns inward, trying to satisfy the self, and it never finds anything big enough to do so. Faith works outward, into love of God which grows ever more full the more we experience it.

Finding Rest from Desires

There is a simple way out of covetousness. Jesus provides that way out in an invitation to all of us:

> *Come to me, all you who are weary and burdened, and I will give you rest. Take my yoke upon you and learn from me, for I am gentle and humble in heart, and you will find rest for your souls. For my yoke is easy and my burden is light (Matthew 11: 28-30).*

165

Jesus tells us that when we come to him, setting God's will before our desires, he will give us rest from the weight and loneliness of our futile efforts to work out our own happiness. Can we understand that as physical rest? Probably. Make no mistake: any effort to appease human desires will eat a person up. The rat race of life chews up people and spits them out as garbage. It is easy to get caught in that rat race. When we turn our eyes to God, we can step out of those struggles. We can rest in God's arms. But I also think Jesus means rest as *peace*—a sense of calm well-being and satisfaction, the same rest God spoke of in Eden when he rested on the Sabbath. It is a rest of the heart. How do we obtain that rest? Jesus tells us to take his yoke upon us.

In biblical times, a yoke was a wooden harness that fit over the shoulders of *two* animals. It was used to fit them together so they could share in pulling the load. Jesus doesn't call us to shoulder a bunch of rules through life, he calls us to *his side*. He says, "Take *my* yoke," meaning that he is already in the other side of the yoke. He calls us to walk alongside him, to let him help us pull the load. Jesus gives us rest because he helps us pull through life's burdens. Jesus, the almighty God himself, is at our side, pulling us through.

He calls the yoke "easy." An "easy" yoke is one that fits perfectly. If a yoke did not fit properly, it would rub against the animal, making sores and bruises. Jesus promises that his yoke will not bruise us, but give us peace and rest. Here we discover the mysterious and miraculous working of grace. One submits to a yoke, but in so doing discovers all the help one could ever need. The mystery of God's gracious goodness befuddles human expectation.

It may seem that we must give up so much. What we give up, however, is the terror of loneliness and insufficiency. The *burden of grace* is to acknowledge need, to crack the dam of self-sufficiency and reliance on our own futile efforts. The *glory of grace* lies in the fact that it turns our lives around into purposeful, satisfied, happy partnerships with an almighty, loving God.

REFLECTIONS

1. The author describes the sin of coveting as "a desire for something that doesn't belong to us." He expands: "Here is the pattern we have observed in all the commandments: a longing for something that can satisfy our yearnings and desires."

   Think about those yearnings and desires for a minute. Do you think that such human longing is a universal thing? Is there, in everyone, a longing for satisfaction? What evidence makes you feel this way?

   What is the source of such longing? Why do so few people seem really satisfied?

2. Coveting is sometimes called the "secret sin" because it springs from deep in the heart. But is this true? How would coveting eventually reveal itself?

3. The commandment lists examples of coveting from Old Testament times: a house, wife, servants, ox, donkey. What examples could we list today?

4. In the recollection of "Uncle Bert's Candy Store," the author (as a child) receives what he is craving—candy— but is left feeling "a lot worse than when I was devouring it. And it wasn't long before the old craving returned once again." How does this illustration capture the experience of coveting?

   Why can we never be satisfied by the things we covet— even if those things become ours?

5. According to the author, "this last commandment, together with the first, are sometimes described as bookends to all the others. Both have to do with where we direct our heart's desire; all the other commandments deal with actions that stem from that desire."

If this is true, how could faith be considered a "cure" for coveting?

6. Read again the beautiful invitation from Jesus that concludes this chapter. Read it aloud to yourself:

Come to me, all you who are weary and burdened, and I will give you rest. Take my yoke upon you and learn from me, for I am gentle and humble in heart, and you will find rest for your souls. For my yoke is easy and my burden is light (Matthew 11:28-30).

How does that invitation make you feel? In what way is Jesus' invitation a cure for the sin of coveting?

How is Jesus' "yoke" a reflection of the Ten Commandments as we have been considering them—a guide to happiness from a God who loves us dearly?

11

In the Potter's House

I n the second and third chapters of the book of the Revelation, the apostle John records letters to seven churches in the province of Asia. The most fearful of those letters is to the church in Laodicea.

This church, located in a wealthy city renowned for its rich clothing industry, was not unlike many modern churches. Its problem was complacency—its sin, self-sufficiency. Because of their great wealth, the Laodiceans believed they needed no one. Because of their smugness, they even came to believe that they didn't need the Lord. They had grown lukewarm in their Christian faith, letting it subside into mere habit. Consequently, the fearful judgment of the Lord rests upon them: "So, because you are lukewarm—neither hot nor cold—I am about to spit you out of my mouth" (Revelation 3:16). Such people stand forever on the outskirts of the Holy of Holies—consumed by self and destitute of grace.

Yet, the theme of the entire book of Revelation, with all its dire warnings and terrifying prophecy, is nothing less than grace. The book was written, as the introductory verses make clear, for the blessing of Jesus' people, and as evidence of the Lord's grace and peace. So, too, the threat against Laodicea was offset by an offer of peace.

Jesus offers a beautiful, powerful image of himself in the verses of this letter to the Laodicean Christians, using terms readily comprehended: "Those whom I love I rebuke and discipline. So be earnest, and repent. Here I am! I stand at the door and knock. If anyone hears my voice and opens the door, I will come in and eat with him, and he with me" (Revelation 3:19-20). This eternal Lord also stands at the door of our lives and knocks, and he himself is also the door to eternal life. By admitting him into our lives, we also pass through his doorway into eternal life.

Like the Revelation letter to Laodicea, the Ten Commandments carry with them both warning and promise. They, too, are a doorway into a life blessed with God's protection and promise. Because Jesus kept these commandments in our

170

stead, and because he died for our sins against them, we can enter into a loving relationship that will achieve its full glory in eternal life.

When one looks back upon the Ten Commandments after a period of intensive study, one sees certain clear truths that stand out like a kind of bas-relief against the solid structure of Scripture. In particular, I am struck by the centrality of God and the rewards of righteousness that are so clearly etched into their words.

The Centrality of God

Foremost in the Ten Commandments is the powerful centrality of God in all of life. Each commandment emphasizes that God is to be our first choice. Everything else will fall into place if we make that choice. God won't abandon us.

Any violation of the commandments, conversely, is really a choosing against God. We violate any commandment when we choose our own desires or needs rather than the will of God. The result of that choice is an alienation from God and a dissatisfaction with self. We can never satisfy our own desires and needs; it's like trying to feed a fire. The more wood we throw on, the hotter it burns. What the fire leaves behind, finally, is nothing but ashes—the loneliness of the person choosing his own way rather than God's.

There is an interesting event in Israelite history that illuminates our understanding of how the commandments bring us into a closer walk with God. It took place at the end of the Israelites' exile under Babylonian and then Persian rule. Nehemiah, a Jew who had been a trusted cupbearer to the king of Persia, requested and received permission to lead a group of Jews back to Jerusalem to begin rebuilding the destroyed temple and the city walls.

The Old Testament book of Nehemiah records the Israelites' long and lonely effort to rebuild the city of God. Nehemiah directed his people in the construction. Finally, once again, the people had a safe place to worship God, but they had yet to make God the center of their lives.

Nehemiah realized this. He assembled all the people. He directed a priest named Ezra to read the law of God to the gathered crowd. As Ezra read, Nehemiah was forced to stop. The people were weeping loudly. They wept out of joy over hearing once again the beautiful words of God's law, and they wept as they realized how they had forsaken that law. Ezra stopped them and called for a spirit of celebration. "Do not grieve," he told them, "for the joy of the Lord is your strength." The people went out rejoicing, "because they now understood the words that had been made known to them." Understanding the law, they also understood God's love for them. And they, in turn, recovered their love for God, celebrating it with jubilation.

After seven days of celebration, the Israelites assembled once again—this time to make confession. They had discovered God's love for them and had rejoiced in that love. But now they needed to make themselves right with God. As they did so, they heard from the priest a powerfully moving statement of God's deep compassion and love. The conclusion to that sermon begins in Nehemiah 9, verse 32, where the priests proclaim: "Now therefore, O our God, the great, mighty and awesome God, who keeps his covenant of love . . ." God's commandments *are* a covenant of his love for us. The centrality of God in our lives is the unfailing rock of compassion and loving-kindness.

After the Israelites heard the revelation of God's loving law as recorded in Nehemiah, they understood where God stood in relation to them—in a posture of love and blessing. They saw also that they had to take a stand for God. So chapter 10 of Nehemiah records that the people "separated themselves from the neighboring peoples for the sake of the Law of God." They pledged themselves with "an oath to follow the Law of God . . . and to obey carefully all the commands, regulations and decrees of the Lord our God" (Nehemiah

10:28, 29). They saw the alternatives, and aligned themselves with God.

The Reward of Righteousness

The Old Testament records over and over again the rewards that come with putting God first. Isaiah 48:18 expresses God's promise, even in words to a nation that had forsaken him: "If only you had paid attention to my commands, your peace would have been like a river, your righteousness like the waves of the sea." These promises are echoed by Jesus, who says, in John 14:27, "Peace I leave with you; my peace I give you. I do not give to you as the world gives. Do not let your hearts be troubled and do not be afraid."

Such passages tell us the blessings of faithfulness. We look to the Ten Commandments for guidance, not because we hope to gain merit or favor by keeping them. We will always fail in our efforts. But, because Jesus has kept those commandments for us, and because he has won for us a place in God's family, we respond in loving obedience to such divine love.

It is no historical accident, I believe, that Jesus preached his most famous sermon in Matthew 5 from a mountain. It is the perfect parallel to the Ten Commandments given on Mount Sinai. Jesus gives a pattern for Christian living, and he tells us, in that passage from which we have quoted so many times, and here quote fully for the first time:

Do not think that I have come to abolish the Law or the Prophets; I have not come to abolish them but to fulfill them. I tell you the truth, until heaven and earth disappear, not the smallest letter, the least stroke of a pen, will by any means disappear from the Law until everything is accomplished. Anyone who breaks one of the least of these commandments and teaches others to do the same will be called least in the kingdom of heaven, but whoever practices and teaches these commands will be called great in the kingdom of heaven" (Matthew 5:17-19).

Here Jesus penetrates to the reality of human experience. He tells us how breaking or keeping the commandments begins in an action of the heart. And Jesus also drives directly to the core of God's law: Whom will you serve? What do you love?

Abiding by God's commandments—through the power that Jesus gives—creates a two-way awareness of love. It affirms God's love for us, and also our love for God. I find this idea beautifully expressed in the apostle John's great letter about faith and love:

> *This is how we know that we love the children of God: by loving God and carrying out his commands. This is love for God: to obey his commands. And his commands are not burdensome, for everyone born of God overcomes the world. This is the victory that has overcome the world, even our faith. Who is it that overcomes the world? Only he who believes that Jesus is the Son of God? (1 John 5:2-5).*

Here John describes our obligation to obey God as an expression of our love for him, *and* he explains the source of power that enables us to show such love: the new lives that we have been given by the grace of Jesus. Through Jesus' love for us we are empowered to show our love for God and for one another.

The Lesson of the Potter's House

A wonderful illustration of our relationship with God is drawn from a scene that was common in biblical times and can still be observed today: a potter working with clay. What becomes clear as we watch any potter working is the fact that the potter loves the clay that is being transformed—squeezed, spun, shaped, and molded—into a vessel. Like a potter, God lovingly molds and forms us—his clay.

That image of the potter and the clay is worth a closer look at the end of our study, for it also is an image that runs throughout the Bible. It appears poignantly in Jeremiah 18:1-4:

> *This is the word that came to Jeremiah from the Lord: "Go down to the potter's house, and there I will give you my message." So I went down to the potter's house, and I saw him working at the wheel. But the pot he was shaping from the clay was marred in his hands; so the potter formed it into another pot, shaping it as seemed best to him.*

Several things are striking about that story Jeremiah tells. The potter and his clay was an image of God's relationship with his creation—us. Can you see the analogy between God as the potter and humans as his clay? In biblical times, a potter would be working at a wheel he propels round and round by his feet. If we are the clay, then the wheel represents our environment—our lives. It is the life into which God has placed us and to which he has called us. God has control of the wheel. He directs our lives and the entire circumstances of our lives. All those events go into the shaping of a beautiful vessel—a creature made by God's loving hands.

Now, there doesn't appear to be anything special about the clay in Jeremiah's story. In fact, it's likely quite common clay. Only the working of the master potter gives the clay beauty and strength. But verse 4 says that the "clay was marred in his hands." What does this part of the story mean? In this life on the wheel, even under the master's touch, some foreign substance may intrude and damage the vessel.

Each one of us is marred and flawed by sin. We cannot blame God, the Master Potter, for the flaw; it is in our sinful human nature and in the choices we make. But the clay is still in the hands of the Master Potter.

The second thing we observe about Jeremiah's potter is that, even though the clay is flawed, the potter does not give up on it. If the clay itself were impure, we would expect the potter to throw it out. Such a thing any human potter would have to do. But this is the Master Potter, the loving God. And God Almighty can take that impure lump and remold it, remake it into a new creation.

Some years ago there was a popular slogan in Christian circles: "God doesn't make junk." As with all slogans, that's only part of the story. God also takes the junk in our lives, rids us of it, and makes us into something eternally precious.

Yet, how does our Potter-God do this? And why?

The two questions can be answered in one word: love. The vessel is shaped from *within* and from *without*. One hand inside and the other outside, that's the way the Potter works. The gentle hands of the Potter work within our lives to shape us and work outside our lives to protect and guide us. Those hands that shape us so tenderly from within and without bear the imprint of nails. Those hands have bled in order to hold us so. They won't cast us aside. The Potter endured the cross on Calvary in order to hold us just so.

The Ten Commandments are part of the way that our loving Potter shapes us. They are both a guide and a protection for us as we are formed into God's beautiful vessels. If we have learned anything about the commandments, that is it.

These laws, which appear upon first glance to be merely a list of rules, function dynamically in the Christian life. They provide a means of walking in a loving relationship with God, a relationship that has already been assured for us by Jesus. They direct our path through life. And, finally, they are a means of protection for us, a carapace of God's love around us, until we walk, finally, on the streets of heaven. Then, the perfect and holy relationship that the commandments point to will be fulfilled perfectly and there will be no need for commandments.